Mervyn's Lot

Also by Mervyn Matthews
Mila and Mervusya: A Russian Wedding

Mervyn Matthews

Mervyn's Lot

seren

Seren is the book imprint of
Poetry Wales Press Ltd
Nolton Street, Bridgend, Wales
www.seren-books.com

ISBN 1-85411-319-4

A CIP record for this title is available from
the British Library

*The publisher works with the financial assistance of the
Arts Council of Wales*

Printed in Plantin by CPD Wales, Ebbw Vale

CONTENTS

LIST OF ILLUSTRATIONS

PREFACE

And the stately ships go on
To their haven under the hill;
But O for the touch of a vanished hand,
And the sound of a voice that is still!

Alfred Lord Tennyson

Life is not only a matter of great adventure. Thrills and dangers may have a place in the path one has trodden, but for most people, most of the time, life is made up of familiar activities in ordinary situations: meetings with near and dear, or less so, and workaday problems. Matters like these, though striking on a personal plane, are of little import in the world at large. Nevertheless, accounts of them can surprise and make absorbing reading, even though they lack blood and thunder. Hence the perennial popularity of writers like Marcel Proust – their writing affords more subtle pleasures.

As a boy living in the crowded back streets of Swansea, an industrial town in South Wales, I did, indeed, witness some cataclysmic events – not least the massive bombing during the Second World War. But when the drone of the German bombers had died away, and the dust settled over the ruins, my attention returned to my own circumstances, and the dramas being played out in the family around me. They are recounted here.

This book is, in a sense, a small dream fulfilled, for I have always wanted to tell the tale of my boyhood years. Even then I had a feeling that I would eventually do so, and for this reason kept diaries for months on end. Some of the narrative in these pages is based on what I wrote then, between the ages of nine and fourteen or so. In addition, I have some family papers, many photographs and, of course, my own recollections.

Fortunately, I am writing when only in my late sixties. The older generations have passed away, but some of my contemporaries are still here, and have been able to help me recall the past. Many of my boyhood haunts can still be revisited, too. Memory fades, but some facts may stand out more clearly. And as one's experience of life grows, there is a richer field for comparison.

I have avoided any significant fictionalisation, because I believe it has no place in autobiography. At the same time some conversations

7

have had to be reconstituted (to repeat the term I used in my recent memoir *Mila and Mervusya*): some events have been a little displaced in time, to help the flow of the narrative; and others have been omitted, as inclusion would have made the book too cumbersome. A few names, alas, have been changed to avoid possible embarrassment. Beyond that I would ask the readers' indulgence for any factual errors which may come to their notice. My boyhood diary extracts have been meticulously copied, retaining the original grammar and (betimes) peculiar spelling.

May I add a word of thanks to those who read the manuscript and offered advice, including Mick Felton of Seren, Harry Willetts at Oxford and John Lewis, who is mentioned in the text.

I trust the reader will enjoy reading this book as much as I enjoyed writing it.

Mervyn Matthews

ONE

BOMBED OUT

We reached the top of Lamb Street just as the sun was rising over the dark sandstone wall of Cwmfelin tin-plate works at the bottom. Before us – my Mother and me – was a scene of unbelievable destruction. I was just eight years old and was astonished to find that the little sloping street with its terraced, working class houses where I had spent most of my life had been half destroyed by one of the German bombs dropped on Swansea the night before.

We had not been there while the air raid was on. We had slept at my Grandmother's, a mile away in the Hafod, as we did on most moonlit nights when raids were likely. It was further from Cwmfelin, and safer. We had started back after supper, when the 'all clear' went. The streets were unlit (the black-out was on) though red glows in the sky spoke of fire: and although it was late, a great number of people were afoot. What a strange night this is, I thought. We were just crossing the Hafod Bridge which carried the main road over the Cwm valley, when a man's figure loomed through the darkness. You could just make out that he was slim, and wore a workman's cloth cap.

"Billie," my Mother called out. "Billie! Is that you?"

Despite the gloom, my parents recognised one another instantly. My Father was on his way to Gran's to give us the bad news before starting his ten-to-six shift on the docks.

"Lamb Street has copped it," he said. "There's no point in going over there. Best go back to your Mother's, and go over to the house tomorrow morning. I'll meet you there when I come off work."

So we expected the street to be damaged – but not as much as it was. A few of the houses at the top were more or less intact, but much of the street was in ruins. Our house was in the middle; what was it going to be like? My Mother led me quickly down the pavement, now strewn with debris; there was a strange smell of damp plaster everywhere. Neither of us said anything, we just looked. Mrs. Bennett, our next door neighbour, whose buoyant smile was so familiar to me, ran up to meet us, her eyes filled with tears. Perhaps it was this, more than the actual destruction, that disturbed me most. I had never seen her crying.

"It's terrible," she sobbed. "They say Miss Preistly and some of the people living at the bottom of the street have been buried in their Anderson shelter. No one knows whether they are alive or dead."

We reached number 51. It was still standing, but there was a lot of damage. All the windows had been blown out, and the front door was askew on its hinges. This I found surprising, because front doors were sort of solid and for ever. My Mother went in to see what it was like.

"Stay outside, Mervyn," she said. "It might be dangerous." I found, as I waited, that if I looked up from a certain spot on the camber of the road, I could see the sky through holes in the roof on either side. That was most peculiar, too. When my Mother let me in I found a strange mixture of familiar corners and parts made unrecognisable by bomb damage – mainly fallen plaster.

Out in the street, the morning wore on. There were people everywhere, trampling through the dust, calling out to one another, starting to salvage what they could. The sound carried with unnatural clarity through the empty window frames. The local ARP warden, a cheerful little man who lived further down the street, organized a roll-call to see how many people were missing. Somebody said it was about eight. After a while ambulances arrived to rescue the people who had been buried. The ARP man went up and down the pavement, telling everyone to keep indoors, because bodies would be carried out. I was desperate to watch, but they wouldn't let me. When we were allowed out again, the neighbours told us that two people in Miss Priestly's shelter had been suffocated, and a little girl of three whom we knew had been blinded for life. Her father got the news later that morning when he came home from nightwork. Some of the people who were in the shelter had just gone there to keep one another company.

Margery Bennett, who was a couple of years older than I, ventured into our passage with another bit of startling news: the Salvation Army was giving tea and chocolate wafers on Carmarthen Road, *free*. I could not believe my ears, and rushed down to find out. Sure enough, a van was parked there, and women in the familiar black bonnets were filling mugs from white enamelled pitchers. The ration of Kit Kat was real enough, and for a moment my thoughts were lost in the taste of sweet tea and chocolate. For years after, whenever I thought of the Salvation Army, the memory of the jugs and silver packets came to mind. Perhaps the women who handed them out had been bombed themselves.

My Father arrived as soon as his night work finished. He and my Mother decided on the spot that we couldn't live in our house any more, the dilapidation was too great. The furniture would have to be moved out and we would have to go to my Gran's. As a matter of fact, a man with a lorry was already in the street, loading someone else's. My Father arranged for him to come and take ours the following afternoon. We would get it out on the pavement ready. My parents spent the rest of the day sorting things out, and wondering how they were going to get all our stuff into Gran's small dwelling. I just hung around, watching.

The next day was grey, but not actually raining. As it happened, it was rent day, and in the morning Mr. Thomas, who owned our house and a few others in the same row, sent his daughter, my Auntie Kate, around to collect the cash: no bank accounts in those days. Aunt Kate was a forceful woman with an unsightly wart on her chin. She may well have heard that Lamb Street had been bombed, but she came anyway. A nasty exchange was inevitable.

"You haven't come for the rent, have you?" said my Mother, though the reason for Auntie Kate's arrival was obvious enough.

"Well, you're still living here, aren't you?" answered Auntie Kate, doggedly.

"We won't be much longer, it's a ruin!"

"The money is due, anyway!"

Whether she got her nine shillings or so I do not know, but the incident was never forgotten, and used with dreadful effect in family feuds long afterwards. I remember Mr. Thomas as a quiet, white-haired old gentleman who regularly refused to do repairs. Another of his indelible sins was to have given my Father sixpence for unblocking the kitchen drain out the back.

Eventually my Father got most of our furniture, including a cheap bedroom suite and an even cheaper parlour suite, out onto the pavement, ready for the lorry. We waited, hoping the rain would hold off. In the end we gave up – there was no rain, but no lorry either, and as darkness fell we carried everything back into the house. A day or so later my father found other transport, and the furniture was moved – some, for a weekly payment, to one of Gran's next-door neighbours, some to a big cupboard at my rich Auntie Annie's in Treboeth, and the rest to Gran's in the Hafod.

That was how my childhood in Lamb Street ended.

* * *

My Mother, naturally enough, was at the centre of my universe. She was devoted, caring and protective, as a mother should be, and it was thus that I saw her. Sometimes she would wrap me up in a blanket and sit me on her knee at the bottom of the stair just as a sign of affection, I liked it but was a bit ashamed, too. She made no secret of the fact that she had wanted a girl, but that was a matter completely beyond redemption, and she seemed quite satisfied with what she got. Only in later years did I come to appreciate the hardships she had had to surmount before she became a mother. She had managed to stay at a secondary school and matriculate, despite the fact that my Gran was very poor. (It took me years, of course, to understand what she meant by "matriculation.) She had learned to play the piano by ear – quite beautifully – and was obviously the cleverest of Gran's four children, the others being my Auntie Annie, my Auntie Olive and my Uncle Gilbert, (Auntie Kate's husband).

My Mother was pretty, brown-haired and slightly built: "I was such a pretty little thing when I was young" she would tell me, clicking her teeth in her own, peculiar way. "I was my Father's little favourite, and your Uncle Gilbert loved me, too. I was a really dainty dancer."

But I was a late child, and saw nothing of that. After giving birth to me, she had suffered a collapse of the ligaments in her feet, and became very flat-footed. She was constantly bandaging her instep 'to get support', so I saw her feet often. In fact, I always feared that one of her toes would come off. Strangely enough, despite her music and matriculation, there was no trace of refinement or elegance in her bearing (though I could not appreciate it at the time). She lacked any clothes sense, and usually donned shapeless dresses. She was careless about her nails, and never learned any table manners. Sometimes, instead of using a glass, she would take a swig straight from the bottle of Tizer's Orange, our favourite pop.

I soon realised, however, that in terms of behaviour she was not like the other women in Lamb Street. She did not stand on the pavement, arms folded, and gossip for hours; she didn't go into other people's houses; and she had no real friends among the neighbours. Once, when we went on a street trip to Pyle Corner, she did not join in the singing, and I chided her for not doing so: "Ma, why aren't you singing like the other mothers?" Reluctantly, she struck up.

"I always felt different from other people, Mervyn," she once confided. As it was, I took this for granted – her education and piano-playing seemed to be sufficient explanation. Many years were to pass before the reasons for her isolation became wholly clear to me.

I have no doubt that she passed the same lonesome attitude on to me. There was my first Guy Fawkes night, for example. The children in the street spent an exciting day gathering anything that would burn, to make a bonfire, and fabricating a communal Guy from rags and old garments. But I did not join them: my Mother helped me to make my own Guy in the kitchen, a grotesque figure with a paper face and old woollen socks for feet. Later that night, when the bonfire was bright and roaring, and the street dummy disintegrating in flames, she helped me to carry my Guy down, and toss him onto the fire. We were indeed different.

My Father, lean and handsome, was much more sociable, but he, too, considered himself to be above the crowd. Perhaps that's what originally brought them together. As I found later, they had been genuinely in love at the time of their marriage. Before my Mother's feet gave out, they enjoyed floating over the ballroom floor together, and had shared at least one happy holiday camping in Gower. My Father had no interest in literature – I cannot remember him ever reading a story to me – but he did once compose a poem (more accurately, a jingle) for my Mother. It was entitled 'Billie's Thoughts' and was quite possibly the only verse ever penned by a Swansea docker:

> Tramping along in the month of May
> Feeling so happy and rather gay,
> The warmth of the sun, the green of the field,
> Something that no other season can yield.
> I whistle a song as I tramp along,
> Everything radiates — nothing seems wrong.

Yet it would be difficult to imagine a more fundamentally ill-matched pair. My Father really wanted nothing more than good food (which my Mother provided), someone to wash his working clothes, and a home at minimum cost where he could rest between his shifts and daily beer-and-snooker sessions at the Swansea Labour Club and Institute, not to mention other pubs near the dock entrance. Unlike my Mother, he had been taught rather fastidious manners, and despite his manual job clung dodgedly to a feeling of social superiority. Thinking back, I can hardly remember him having the slightest flicker of interest in family life, apart from the occasional Sunday evening walk, or a brief outing to the Mumbles. On the sole occasion he took us to Limeslade Bay the trip was spoilt by his wanting to get back to the Club as fast as possible.

My Mother, despite her dislike of housework, craved a proper home life with genuine affection. She abhorred pubs and beery conviviality, and could not adapt to his habits. Every evening when he was not at work my Father would don a smart suit, with a waist-coat and heavy gold watch chain, and go out, leaving the two of us at home by the fire. He quickly came to regret the marriage, but my Mother, I believe, never forgot the debonair young man of the 'thirties, nor lost hope of living happily with him.

As a result of all of this, there was constant tension in the house, in fact, hardly a day passed without a row.* Many of the parental quarrels were about money. A strong working-class convention dictated that a husband should not tell his missus how much he earned, and my Father, despite his quality suits and social preten-sions, strictly adhered to this principle. My Mother got about three pounds a week to cover everything, but suspected there had been seven or eight in the wage packet. To be fair, she never wasted a penny, as she did not smoke, drink or gamble, and spent little on clothes. Matters were not helped, either, by my Father's habit of giving money to other children in the family, just to show off.

The other great source of rows, as I saw it, was his attachment to the Labour Club and Institute in Wind Street. My Mother suspected that a lot of his money went into the till of that estab-lishment. He always returned home late, after it had closed, though I never once saw him drunk. As his rows with a resentful wife got worse, he sought refuge there ever more readily. He would some-times mischievously hint, when we were all together in the kitchen, that my Mother complained because she was not 'all there' – which invariably provoked another squabble.

I do, however, remember a few lovely occasions when my parents were not being unpleasant to one another. My Mother would call my Father 'Billie', and he would respond by being kind and sincere, rather than sarcastic. One morning I went downstairs to find the fire already roaring in the grate (it was usually lit much later) and both of them actually smiling at one another. What a wonderful moment that was.

* * *

---

* A defect in English spelling prevents visual distinction between the words for quarrelling, alignment, and propelling a boat. The first, alas, is usually the most apposite in these pages.

My Father was a docker, more precisely a 'coal trimmer', which meant that he loaded coal into ships. His work cast a gritty shadow on our whole manner of living. He came home black, like a miner, and his working clothes had to be washed daily. Nobody in Lamb Street had a hot-water system, let alone a bath, so my Father's arrival was always preceded by the boiling of iron kettles on the kitchen fire. He washed in a zinc bath in the wooden lean-to behind the house. Trimmers did irregular shifts, depending on the ship movements, so sometimes I did not see him for days on end. I was always being told to be quiet because he was asleep upstairs.

The coal-trimmers considered themselves to be a sort of elite among manual labourers, which fitted my Father's assumed superiority. Before the war coal exports were very important in Swansea, and the trimmers had an agreement with ship owners whereby they received not a wage, but a percentage of the cost of coal loaded. In this way they reckoned to do considerably better than men on fixed pay, and indeed, until the war stopped exports, they enjoyed a relatively good income.

My Father's love of refinement meant that he dressed with care, never used bad language, and strange though it might seem, was very sensitive about his hands, which were at once gnarled and delicate. He wrote quite neatly, and was for many years Secretary and a valued member of the Coal Trimmers' Committee. The deliberations of this body took place on a Sunday morning, when my Father would leave the house attired in a blue pin-striped suit and slim black shoes, with perhaps a smart overcoat and trilby. The committee, need I add, met in close proximity to the beer pumps of the Labour Club, one of the very few places where alcohol was available on that day.

My Father's ideal of gentility was maintained against truly hellish conditions at work. I well remember the only occasion he took me on board ship to show me what it was like. What a thrill I had going up the rickety ladder, and clambering onto the iron deck. In no time at all we were approached by a tall Indian sailor in a dirty coal-smeared turban: such headgear was never seen in the streets of Swansea, and I was quite overcome. The man underneath gave me a murky smile.

"How many children?" he asked.

My Father was never one to tell the truth when he could manage something more spectacular.

"Ten," he replied, showing him ten fingers. The Indian was obviously impressed.

After that we went 'below' to see the trimmers at work. Trucks filled with coal were shunted out onto a sort of gantree above the quay-side, and tipped into an enormous iron shute leading down into the ship's hold, or bunker, as the case might be. The coal, sometimes in huge lumps, came thundering down into a confined space below decks. It had to be spread evenly, or 'trimmed', so that the ship did not list at sea: the trimmers did this with the help of shovels and large boards, mostly as it poured in. One man, chosen by lot, had to stand on deck and regulate the tipping, with shouts and a whistle. It could be dark below, and the men sometimes worked by the light of long, tallow candles, bending down as the level of the coal rose and headroom was reduced. The air was thick with coal dust which swirled and glinted near the flames.

Given these conditions, coal-trimmers could expect only illness and lung disease as they got older. The fact that my Father had such an awful, if well-paid, job was always a matter of sorrow on his side of the family: and although my Grandfather had been a founder member of the Coal Trimmers' Association, both he and my Grandmother, or Gamma, as I called her, had wanted my Father, always known in the family by his full name of 'William Alfred', to do better in life. Their house in Osterley Street, St Thomas, was almost middle-class. I often wondered why my Father had chosen coal-trimming: it was not thrust upon him, and a trimmer's 'cap' was not easy to get. He had in fact started life as a telegram boy, and switched. I think the pay, access to the club, and the irregular hours attracted him. Earlier, I was told, he had had Saturday afternoons free for the football match. He later regretted his choice, but lacked the initiative to change. Even when I was a child he urged me to get an office job in which I wouldn't have to 'work hard', as he put it.

Trimmers had to provide their own tools, and I was always interested in the tough but simple implements my Father brought home for repair – large, shining shovels with long handles, lacking the cross-piece found on ordinary garden spades. My Father also made hangers for the tallow candles. For this he used strips of metal, bent to fit the wax stalks, with sliding collars and loops which allowed them to be suspended from a convenient bulkhead. Oil skins were another essential thing, and one of my Father's regular duties was to tar these peculiar garments for use when he was on deck. Like all trimmers, he had a couple of large tarpaulin-covered chests in which he kept his belongings at the dockside. Together, that is, with any useful objects he could pick up.

Indeed, pilfering was regarded by the coal-trimmers as part and parcel of their job. We never heard of anyone who was caught – least of all my Father. Despite a rigorously honest upbringing, he never hesitated to boast about his acquisitions. "I got it off the dock, son," he would say, with his slightly twisted smile. "I stole it." The thieving always made my Mother and me very uneasy, for it was quite outside our family ethic as well. There were many small marine fittings, curiously-shaped hooks, knobs and brackets. Pints of the drabbest paint you could imagine – brown, buff and a lugubrious mauve – found their way into the toolshed down the garden, and then onto our woodwork. The use of a mysterious substance called 'driers' meant that it took days, rather than weeks, to go hard.

One day my Father staggered into the house carrying part of a carcass of beef with the first whiff of decay about it. He loved salting meat, so that it would keep longer: this particular piece, however, only led to another row with my Mother, who said it was uneatable. On another occasion a number of brass Catholic madonnas, with dangerously spiked haloes, made a miraculous appearance in the parlour. God knows where my Father got them from, but they had no beneficial influence on our household. Other such items which came our way from the docks included occasional flat-fish and cutlets, per favour of Mr. Bennett, who worked down the fish market. I don't think my Mother ever refused those.

* * *

My relations with my Father, like most small boys', varied from one day to another, depending partly on the state of play between him and my Mother, who in my eyes was always right. But in many ways I liked and admired him, too. He had signed up for army service in the First World War at 17, while still under age, and had found himself in the trenches only three months later. He had served as a signaller, been gassed, and was wounded five times, with scars to show it. Of seven young men from the locality he was the only one to survive, and was something of a local hero. This certainly bolstered his image in my eyes. I was also very impressed by his handyman skills, his careful table manners (which I imitated), and his avoidance of bad language. My Mother had a small stock of unseemly epithets, strictly excluding anything to do with sex, of course. At Gamma's in St. Thomas, he was always an object of open admiration: William Alfred could do no wrong.

So in some ways we co-operated. He taught me to step-dance, and we sometimes practised together on the patterned oil cloth in a corner of the kitchen. I can still well remember my Mother's rare, approving gaze. I agreed to put his slippers in front of the fire of an evening, so that they would be nice and warm when he came home from the Club. Sometimes, on a Saturday morning, he would take me into town on the yellow tram: I particularly liked sitting on the top deck. "Why don't they have a driver up here as well, Dad?" I asked him one day. He would buy me sweets and a comic, and perhaps take me to the hairdresser's. "There's smart," he'd say, when the cutting was finished. "Now you've got a lovely parting!"

His presence was essential at Christmas. When I got my first steam engine (a delightful little oscillating machine, with a brass boiler and funnel) we found a pipe was leaking, so it would not work. Without further ado he got his soldering iron out and in minutes the engine was puffing away on the kitchen table. The following year he gave me an excellent deal on my train set. When he took me to the toy shop to choose my Christmas gift, he said Father Christmas would bring me a clockwork Hornby locomotive (the cheaper kind). But I got up on Christmas morning to find an electric locomotive, the *Caerphilly Castle*, awaiting me (though without the tender, because it was too expensive). Something that moved without being wound up was marvellous; I don't think anyone else in the street had one.

What a pleasure it was to play with it on a small circle of track in the front room that Christmas morning, the smoke billowing from the little-used grate, and my parents too involved with household matters to quarrel! Outside in the street an old man passed by, cap in hand, singing loudly, so that people would hear him in their houses. I tore myself away from my train set and ran to the front door, and looked out. "Dad," I cried, "there's a beggar in the street! Can we give him something?" My Father did not respond, and the old man got nothing. For a short while I felt dreadful: how could he be so mean on a Christmas morning?

My Father did, indeed, cause me trouble from time to time. When I was particularly naughty he would threaten me with the thick leather belt which he wore in his working trousers. He was always annoyed when I took my playmates 'out the back', that is, into our narrow garden, which could only be entered through the kitchen. One day I led a small friend through when he was in the middle of his dinner. On seeing my Father the boy hesitated.

"Don't take any notice of him," I chirruped. "It's only my Father."

That particularly annoyed him, and he rose threateningly, unbuckling his belt. I could see what was coming.

"I 'opes your bloody trousers falls down," I shouted as I dodged round the kitchen table. My Mother, who did not mind the swearing, thought it was a great joke, and shielded me behind her apron. I was already developing my own brand of cheek.

The tool shed down the garden was another cause of disagreement. I early developed a love of hand-work, and would gladly have mucked about in it for hours. But my Father stopped me, either because he was afraid I might cut myself, or because he was selfish. Once I crept in when he was at work on the dock, and, to my horror, lost my penknife there. A long search failed to find it, but my Father did: he was annoyed again, but did not give me a hiding. Instead he put a padlock on the door. It was a big event in my little world.

★ ★ ★

The marital storms at No. 51 caused swirls in other family relations. My Father's family were convinced that he had married beneath his station and needed their moral support. I never heard Gamma utter a word of criticism of my Mother, and Uncle Emrys, my Father's younger brother, was everyone's friend: but relations between my Mother and her two sisters-in-law – my Aunties Ethel and Beatrice – were, to say the least, tense. Auntie Ethel had married a real army officer, and was very finicky (or picky, as we said) about everything, including her dresses, which she tailored herself. She believed in Christian Science, and lived in Bridgwater, so she could only send letters. Auntie Beatrice, on the other hand, was a Spiritualist and inveterate do-gooder who resided in Cockett, only a mile or so distant and could turn up on the doorstep. In fact she was the main belligerent, always quarrelling in the belief that as a gifted medium she was Putting Things Right. As a matter of fact, when she got older she began to have nervous breakdowns, and ended up in Cefn Coed, the mental hospital, more than once. She called it 'being ill'.

One day, on my way home from school, I was stopped at the corner by a stout, middle-aged lady whom I dimly recognised as my Aunt. She had called at the house a few days before expressly to tell my Mother that the stew she gave my Father was 'like dishwater', and would she please try and do better. My Mother had taken it badly, so relations between them were under extra strain. Auntie

Beatrice was waiting to give me something. As I gazed at the golden pince-nez on her thin, beaked nose, I was more certain than ever that the bridge of it had been worn down by the spring clip.

She bent over me and her watery eyes filled with tears.

"I been ill again, son," she whispered gently, "but I wants to give you a little present. I can't come to your house because of your Mother. She don' understand, son. I only tries to Put Things Right when I sees they are wrong."

So I arrived home feeling rather guilty myself, with a new book of bible stories under my arm. What a strange way, I thought, to congratulate a boy on his birthday.

On another memorable day I got home to find Gamma sitting in our kitchen, prim as ever, having tea with my Father. This was a unique event, as my Mother's passions were enough to scare away anyone, not only Auntie Beatrice. My Mother happened to be out: I was terrified that she would return before the visitor had left, and cause another upset. Happily, I don't think she ever found out about that visit. She was always intensely curious about relations between her mother-in-law and her husband, and I once saw her use a jet of steam from the iron kettle to open an envelope to my Father addressed in Gamma's hand. Heaven knows what paltry facts she expected to uncover. It was all part and parcel of the family feud.

★ ★ ★

Although I was a lonely child, I had a few chosen friends, of whom the best was John Dermady. He lived across the street, in one of the houses which, unlike ours, had two steps up to the front door. His grandmother lived with them, and my Mother referred to them awesomely as a family that lived in peace. John was a retiring boy, and I could just about beat him in fights; every time I did so his mother would come over to complain. But I knew that despite our friendship John was not wholly to be trusted, because he was a Catholic. My Father had warned me about them. The Catholic Irish had once 'black-legged' on the docks, he said, and they worshiped the Catholic Pope. He hinted that my Auntie Eileen, Uncle Emrys's wife, who went to a Catholic church, was not really reliable either. One day John and his little sister came dancing down the street singing, "We are Roman Catholics." This strange word added another mystical dimension to their religious status.

Further down the street lived a sturdy little boy called Elias

Edwards. I was convinced that he was called 'Lias' because he told lies; in any case, he initiated me into many of the secrets of the neighbourhood. It was he who first took me down to see the Red Cow when it was open, noisy, and smelling of beer. He showed me the great 'lectric transformer behind the green railings over Carmarthen Road. He also taught me how to hang on the backs of lorries as they crawled up our hill, and drop off as they turned the corner, picking up speed. Lias always shrugged off ideas of death and danger. "If they knock you down," he assured me, "they've got to pay!"

Gerald Peachey, a boy from England, made a deep impression on me. He sometimes came to stay with his relatives in Lamb Street for the summer holidays. He was a year or two older than myself, and possessed immense authority. He talked with an English accent, so I was inevitably accused of 'going with' him because he talked funny. He did excellent imitations of a policeman, for which he donned a real police helmet, and would tell stories, drawing pictures of the action at the same time. He told us that he lived in a marvellous town called Scunthorpe, and implied that we were lucky to see him at all in a place like Swansea. His young brother Alan wore a silly knitted suit, and constantly got in our way.

When Gerald came down, I was allowed to help with the horse. The point was that his grandfather, who was thought to be pretty nasty, had a milk-round, and he kept his cart, and the nag which pulled it, in a crumbling stable opposite the Cwmfelin wall. During Gerald's visits I could go into this evil-smelling place and lend a hand with the feed. The main problem in the family (apart from a constant lack of money) was Gerald's eyesight. Young though he was, he wore extremely thick glasses, and a 'specialist' down in Llanelly saw him free of charge. Blindness must have been looming even in those days.

My other main friend was fat, dark-haired Teddy Richards who lived opposite Waun Wen School. Everyone knew he was from a bad home, but rumour had it that somebody in his family had once been mayor of Swansea. One morning, when the rain was pouring down, there was a knock on our door. I ran to open it and found Teddy standing there, soaked to the skin.

"Is your Mother in?" he asked. "My Mother sent me down to see if you had any spare shoes I could borrow."

I looked down and saw that he was barefoot. The road outside the house was gravely, and I wondered how he had got over it – it must have hurt like anything. My Mother was behind me in the passage.

"I'll just have a look, Teddy," she said in a kindly voice. "Come in out of the rain."

I did not have much spare footwear, but my Mother found him a pair, and socks to go with them: being without shoes was considered the ultimate humiliation in Lamb Street. Teddy was a clever boy in the classroom – when he attended.

At the bottom of the street, on the opposite side, lived John Bevan, my main enemy. He was a bit older than I, and bigger. I cannot remember how hostilities started, but dislike was mutual, and he was responsible for an incident which made a clear watershed in my mind. At the bottom of Lamb Street we had a little grocer's shop where I spent my weekly pocket money – a ha'penny – on sweets. I also used to get the Tizer's Orange there, or perhaps a bottle of brown Dandelion and Burdock. One Friday afternoon I was on my way back with the sweets and a heavy bottle when John Bevan rushed up from behind and pushed me. I dropped the bottle, which smashed, and I fell onto it, cutting the palm of my right hand. There was rather profuse bleeding. The sight of blood and the fizzy orange drink running over the gravel terrified me, and I ran into the house screaming. My Mother dashed out to get the ambulance driver who lived down the street, and together they staunched the wound.

The incident was followed by the inevitable confrontation between mothers.

"I would have punished John if it had been any other boy," Mrs. Bevan declared stoutly, "but not for Mervyn!"

I heard no more of the argument, but I was puzzled: what had I done, at my age, for her to say that? Was it because I was already an outsider, who had thrown his own Guy on the bonfire? In any case, the incident affected me deeply, and strengthened my feeling of separation from the other children. I was to keep the scar, with a little bit of Lamb Street grit lodged under it, throughout life; the ambulance man said it should have been stitched, but that would have meant making an expensive visit to the doctor's.

A few other children of my own age have maintained a flickering existence in my memory. John Davies, who lived on Waun Wen Road, which I firmly believed to be the steepest road in the world, terrorised me at school until the day I hit him, when it all stopped. Girls, who played hopscotch, and were ridiculed for their frilly knickers, hardly came into the picture at all. My only emotional involvement was a brief affair with a fair-haired creature called Cherry. I can see her now, against a background of bedraggled privet, which suggests that we met in the park at the top of the hill. Her friends said we were 'going together', and I felt a strange tinge of responsibility.

★ ★ ★

The games played in Lamb Street were unending, and ranged from highly energetic ones like chasing and football to conkers, glass marbles and dandies (little pebbles that you tossed and caught on the back of your hand). The girls were always at hopscotch. I was alone in the street in having a four-wheeled vehicle, for my Father had found a primitive pedal car, which he painted buff, and gave me as a present. I liked to push this to the top of the street and race down the pavement, making a terrible clatter. "Stop it!" our neighbour Tilly Fisher (the fattest woman I could imagine) would shout. "You're waking the men up!" Many of them did night work, like my Father.

Exploring the district was another of our pastimes. One afternoon some of us went to Cwmbwrla, where a dirty stream flowed out of the old Coffin Ponds. Somebody, I was told, had once been drowned in them, hence the name. We paddled and fished in the grey water for hours and I returned to Lamb Street with a few tadpoles and a tiny, transparent minnow. My Mother was tearful and distraught: she thought I was lost, and had been on the point of going down the police station. Not saying where you were going, I found, was as bad as getting lost.

I often wondered what lay behind the brown sandstone wall of Cwmfelin works at the bottom of the street. Probably it was an area of wasteland; the smelting shops were further away, but not so far as to make the clash of metal inaudible, nor dim the glare of the furnaces. One morning – I must have been very small – I wandered a long way down Llangyfelach Street, skirting the wall. Suddenly I saw an enormous black tower, wooden, square and windowless, on the other side. I could not, for the life of me, imagine what this dreadful structure was for – it certainly exuded evil. One of the boys once told me it was a torture chamber, and I clung to that belief for many years.

★ ★ ★

Starting school gave me a nasty jolt. I cried hard for most of the first day, and would, no doubt, have cried harder, had I realised how much more was to come. After a breakfast which we had much earlier than usual, my Mother dressed me and put her outdoor coat on. I had never seen her get ready to go out so early, and I was uneasy about the whole thing. We left the house and she led me up the street, which seemed particularly steep that morning, towards Waun Wen School at the top. A few minutes later, after a brief meeting with the head mistress, I found myself in the infants' class; it was a large square room with a blackboard about a foot wide around the walls. I did not know any of the children, nor the lady teacher, and I felt completely out of place.

"Now, babies," said the teacher (we were all pushing six) "if you are very good this morning I shall call you 'boys and girls' instead of 'babies'." That was by way of encouragement. Mercifully, there was a mid-morning break when you could go out and run around the yard. The boys' lavatory, with its tarred wall, was a must. My class-mates, I found, took great delight in peeing games, to see who could do it the highest, or make the most interesting patterns on the wall. One day I went in without looking and actually got my hair wet.

As early as the second day, problems began to arise in the class-room. With the first day safely over, my Mother refused to get up the half hour or so earlier needed to get me off to school on time, so I would invariably arrive to find the classroom door closed, and a hubbub of voices behind it. I would gingerly turn the brass knob just above my head and squeeze in to face our reproachful teacher.

"Late again, Mervyn!" she would cry, as though it were my fault. "Why can't you get to school on time, like everybody else? If you're late again tomorrow we shan't let you draw!"

She was referring to the other problem I was having. Early in the afternoon, after the lunch-break, the children were told to put their arms on their desks and bury their heads for a nap. But there was no way I could doze off, so after a while I was given chalk, and allowed to draw on the black-board. My passion for the steamships my Father was always talking about was already strong, and it was with these that I filled the narrow space, surprising the teachers by the detail I packed in. Tramp steamers, cargo-boats and tankers were all in my repertoire. I had a particular fondness for dredgers and mud-hoppers.

I believe the matter of my lateness got as far as the headmistress, but there was really nothing they could do, so they still let me draw while everyone else slept. The complaints I took home were not heeded, and I continued to be late until I moved up to the next class, when, for reasons which she alone understood, my Mother started getting up earlier.

Standard Two shared the room with another class. A curtain ran along a cord down the middle, and as a result we all had two lessons in one. Our new teacher, a short, fat and jolly lady called Miss Matthews, seemed to take a particular interest in me. (I could never understand why she should have had the same name as us, yet not be related.) She taught us the alphabet, and took us through the first reading books.

My Mother always wanted me to be a 'good scholar', yet she did not provide much back-up at home. Neither she nor my Father ever read anything except a newspaper, and we did not get that regularly. The idea of getting books never entered their heads, unless it was some sort of gift or offer, like the prizes for good attendance from the Sunday School – 'The Hosanna' stories and *The Coral Island*. I was at home with the 'flu when someone brought the latter up from the mission, and my Mother read it to me aloud. It was a book which I came to love, and it is still on my shelf.

Although my Mother did not like house work, she got *Snow White and the Seven Dwarfs* from a Stephenson's Non-Smear Polish offer. The book was particularly exciting, as it had coloured pictures which acquired an eerie depth when you looked at them through celluloid spectacles. A newspaper promotion brought a small set of red-bound volumes, including *The Home Doctor*, *The Home Solicitor* and *Problems of Life*, though they were as yet far beyond my comprehension. That, I think, was the entire stock of books in the house. The first story I ever read by myself (it was about a pirate called Jolly Roger) took up a whole page of the *Beano* comic. I remember thinking, as I sat in the kitchen, "Well, I can read now." School, boring though it was, was having its effect.

In fact, I had been doing quite well, and was soon at the top of the class. After the bombing my Mother took me up to see the Headmaster (the post had changed hands) to tell him about our enforced move to the Hafod. "Sorry Mervyn's going," he said, beaming. "He's doing well at Waun Wen. A sure winner of the Scholarship!"

* * *

I seem to have loved music from a very early age. We kept a large, weak wireless set on the window sill, and we had a wind-up gramophone in a walnut cabinet, with doors which could be opened or closed to regulate the volume. The few records which went with it are, by some incredible chance, also still with me. Gracie Fields's romance with the gentleman in the Tyrolean hat, and her rendering of 'Did Your Mother Come From Ireland?' were among my favourites. My Mother was no doubt responsible for the inclusion of 'A Boy's Best Friend is His Mother', and 'Where is My Wandering Boy Tonight?' in our modest collection.

Occasionally there was music on the wireless. One year, just before Christmas, they started playing a song called 'The Little Boy that Santa Claus Forgot'. Overcome with pity, I wailed whenever I heard it.

"Turn it off, Dad," I would sob. "It's too sad!"

"Don't be silly," my Father would answer. "It's only a song."

And I would have to put up with it.

About the same time I heard my very first live concert performance at school: a little girl called Elizabeth, who was learning the violin, brought her instrument in and played to us. She scraped out a thin, scarcely recognisable melody. I thought it was terrible; I had expected the nice loud sounds I could hear at home.

★ ★ ★

Religion was even more boring than school. Our devotions took place in the Baptist Mission at the bottom of the street. It was one of those little halls which you scarcely noticed, with painted walls, wooden furniture and an iron stove. Attendance for the children's story groups on Sunday afternoon was almost obligatory, a godsend for parents who wanted to have a quiet post-prandial hour in bed. The people in the Mission taught us about God, the Bible, and not swearing or telling lies or stealing. You would, we learned, be punished for your sins, because God saw everything. There were bible story competitions and recitation. Occasionally my Mother took me to an evening service. Once, we went in a little late, and the preaching had started. As she sat down my Mother covered her face with her hand to say a prayer. I was embarrassed and nudged her.

"Ma, he's still talking!" I said.

"Shut up," she hissed angrily. "Can't you see? I'm praying to Gawd!"

I soon discovered that religion was a complicated matter, too. One Sunday evening, before he went to the Labour Club, my Father took us for a walk down to High Street station. There were a lot of people around, a Salvation Army band was playing, and the uniformed Salvationists were collecting money, as usual. Suddenly we heard a shout, and saw a commotion: an old man with a collection box had been knocked down by a car. His cap was lying on the road. Everybody gathered around to help him. I was not allowed to approach, in case there was blood: but how on earth, I thought (my Father always said 'how on earth') could God have allowed that to happen? The old man was helping Him, wasn't he?

The thing called 'bad luck' did not fit in, either. Although there was God, you could bring bad luck on yourself just by doing things by accident, like breaking mirrors. I was horrified one day when I smashed a small framed mirror – my Mother had said that that brought bad luck for seven years. So straight after it happened I picked up the largest pieces I could find and presented them to a boy who lived around the corner. He was glad to have them to play with, for he had not heard the rule.

On another occasion, after a visit to the jewellery counter at Woolworth's, I found I had accidentally walked out with a peacock brooch in my hand. I told my Mother.

"You haven't taken a bird, have you?" she asked, horrified. "Oh, my Gawd, that's the worst thing there is. Back luck! It's the same as stealing! How much was it worth? One and six? Well, there's no point in taking it back now, we'd only look silly. But mind you don't do it again."

Its red glass eye was already glinting at me evilly. When I got home I slipped it into the sideboard drawer, where things normally got lost.

My last visit to the Mission was sad indeed. For reasons which I have quite forgotten, I always hankered after one of the green hymn books we used there. One evening, after the bombing, my Mother and I were finishing a forlorn excursion to collect a few things from our war-damaged house when we saw the caretaker standing outside. I asked whether I could get a hymn book, and he readily agreed. I ventured in. The hall, I found, had been badly hit and the floor was a mass of rubble and broken benches. The familiar smell of damp plaster was there as well, and a strange, empty silence reigned. I picked up one of the worn green volumes, and hurried back out into the street.

* * *

The first break-up in my parents' marriage had occurred when I was a baby only five months old; for reasons never revealed to me, my Father walked out, and was not seen for about a year. He took refuge at Gamma's over in Osterley Street. But as a young boy I was to witness two major confrontations in Lamb Street, both very disturbing.

When I was old enough I was moved from my cot in the front bedroom, where my parents slept, to a bed in the small back bedroom. It was a dark room, with nothing but oilcloth on the floor, and I never really liked it. Some of the parental clashes took place in the dead of night, and my Mother would sometimes come in to sleep with me after they were over.

One night she padded in and told me, though I was half asleep, that my Father had got angry and thrown the grey alarm clock across the room. "I'll sleep with you instead, Mervyn," she said. I was rather surprised, for the clock was important; my Father depended on it to get up for his morning shifts. I was not allowed to touch it, having already, to his consternation, broken the brass timepiece in the kitchen: my Mother would let me play with almost anything. The alarm clock was an interesting one, too – it had levers on the side which gave different kinds of ringing noises, depending on how you liked to be woken up.

Anyway, when I got up next morning I saw it had been placed on the mantelpiece in the kitchen, and had acquired a great big dent. Bickering started again and my Mother mentioned the clock. My Father turned to me, questioningly.

"It was like that before, wasn't it Son?" he said.

I was so surprised by his lying that I couldn't find anything to say. How could he be so untruthful? I think an underlying distrust of his roguery started at that moment, and I never quite lost it.

The most harrowing row of all took place one evening when my Father was sprucing himself up for yet another night out. My Mother, resentful at being left home again, started to nag him. Before I knew what was happening they were involved in a furious bout of fisticuffs, with my Mother screaming. My Father pushed her on to a chair and tried to grab her leg. It was a moment which was to stay with me for ever. The noise was so bad that some neighbours came to the front door to find out what was going on.

"Stop it, Dad, stop it!" I cried, but in vain.

Some time before I had been given a small canvas tent. The poles that went with it had brass sockets at the end, so that one could fit into the other. Desperate to help my Mother, I seized one that was lying around, and walloped my Father with the metal end. The scene was over in a few minutes. The neighbours went off; my Father retreated to the Club, and thereafter to Osterley Street. My Mother, after regaining a degree of composure, dressed and took me to Gran's, as she had done many times before. The marriage had collapsed again.

A few days later my Mother sent me to Osterley Street to reconnoitre and bring back news of the enemy camp. It was my first experience of being a go-between. The door in Gamma's passageway had wine-coloured glass, which threw a red glow. When my Father opened it, I peered at his face in the reflected light: the scar I had made on his cheek had begun to heal. It was some weeks before he returned to Lamb Street, but return he did; nothing changed in his lifestyle, though.

* * *

When they told me we were actually 'at war' I was thrilled: obviously, interesting things were going to happen. My Mother took me over to see Gran the same day, and I danced along the pavement. Everybody said there would be a 'black-out' and 'shortages', and that it would be hard to get meat and vegetables. What fun!

The effects of the hostilities, however, intruded into our lives only gradually. Swansea Corporation, mysterious, but ever-present, put an air-raid siren in Cwmfelin works, and we had to learn the different signals: a rising and falling whine for Danger, and a sustained single note for All Clear. It was a rich, vibrant sound, and I often wondered how it was made. In school, a little later, they gave each pupil a gas mask and taught us how to use it. If you blew the right way you could make it fart, but that was soon forbidden.

Soon the Corporation started providing Anderson air-raid shelters, corrugated iron things that had to be half-buried in the garden. I suppose a few of them are still around today. People who didn't have anywhere to put one were supposed to go to a communal shelter, or find place for a big iron table called a Morrison Shelter that you could crawl into when the siren went.

My Father, an individualist in this, as in other matters, scorned the official solutions. He knew all about the trenches in Flanders, and declared he was going to make his own underground shelter. One day a lorry came to the house and delivered a load of railway sleepers, probably the most bulky things he had ever stolen. With these he constructed, just beyond the blackcurrant bushes, a hefty dug-out, unique, splintery, and probably lethal if hit. It contained a sort of bunk for me, and was lit by coal-trimmers' candles suspended in their metal strips. Everything in it was dreadfully damp. We spent many nights there, called from our beds by the Cwmfelin siren. I would be carried out in my warm 'siren suit', and deposited in the bunk to go back to sleep. The world looked quite different when you started the day by climbing out into the garden, and running into the house for breakfast.

During the ensuing blitzes, the shelter served us in good stead. The first concentrated bombing of Swansea took place on a Sunday night in, I think, September, 1940; we spent it huddled under the sleepers. What a night of terror that was. Waves of bombers came over, dropping stick after stick of whistling bombs. Despite the presence of my parents, fear gripped me every time the engines droned louder. There were the terrible explosions: the earth shook under us. The Germans were obviously aiming for Cwmfelin Works. I would listen to the whistle as the bombs fell, wondering whether one of them was for us. When my parents let me look out, during a lull, I found the sky was red with fire. Neighbours were shouting to one another over the garden walls, trying to guess what had been hit, reassuring one another. In the end I was so frightened that my teeth began to chatter, and they kept on chattering until I fell asleep. Fortunately for us, Lamb Street escaped – on that occasion. It has been my fate to live through several fearful moments in life, but none bad enough to cause the same dental reaction.

Perhaps it was the air raid warnings that brought on one of my earliest nightmares. I was not a privy-orientated child, though I did sometimes watch the water swirling down the brown conical pan which formed the centrepiece of ours. Occasionally, on a disturbed night in the shelter, I would see my Mother, my Father and myself, all in the big double bed, reduced to doll-size, being sluiced round and round towards the dreadful hole at the bottom of the pan. I would wake up with a jolt just before we reached it.

* * *

My Father, as a docker, was not mobilized (he would have been a bit old, anyway). But when he did night work my Mother and I would be left at home alone. My Mother did not like this, so on clear moon-lit nights, when air-raids were most likely, we would go over to Gran's in the Hafod.

This led to difficulties with the chickens, or rather chicks. The Corporation was, it seems, encouraging people to rear edible flesh in their back gardens, and chickens were the most common choice, though some people had rabbits or ducks. They were easy to keep, and it was fun, anyway. You began by picking strong ones, a few days old, at the farm stalls in the market; then you brought them home in a perforated shoe box. If possible you chose perky birds with a feminine look, in the hope that they would be hens and lay eggs. You could check the sex of the bird when you got home by suspending a needle over it, on a thread; if the needle swung in a circle it was a hen, but if the motion was just to and fro you had a cock. I was thought to have a flair for picking hens, and indeed got one or two. My Father, who liked making things, built a wooden coop with a perch in it. I could just about get inside, and on occasion was there when a hen laid an egg, clean and warm, on the dry grass. I began to keep a daily register of their performances. We also had a scraggy white cockerel who learned to answer our call, and sit in my lap when I was on the garden swing.

The well-being of the garden fowl depended to some extent on the life-style of their owners. The Bennetts, next-door, also had chickens, but being a 'shapeless' family, they let them run all over the house.

"They goes around and picks up bits and pieces the kids have dropped," Mrs. Bennett told us, clearly unconcerned by what they left instead.

Their birds, nevertheless, must have led an unsettled existence, for the Bennett marriage contained a robust pugilistic element, and rows were almost as frequent as in our house. I well remember Mrs. Bennett coming in one day with a black eye provided by her husband, Ted.

"Ted done it," she said, "but I bloody well gave him as good as I got."

Their son Terry, who was a few years younger than myself, was very boisterous and one day managed to get their wardrobe to fall over, with him inside it. We heard a terrible bang. His sister Margery ran in to ask if we could help them right it. Our chickens, at least, were in no danger from that sort of thing.

The air-raids, as I say, complicated our poultry rearing. The point was that young chicks could not be left unattended for more than one night; and if for some reason – a daylight raid, perhaps – we were prevented from coming back, they might die. So every time my Mother and I went over to the Hafod we had to wrap them in bits of flannel, and carry them both ways in a cardboard box with a handle. The rigmarole went on for months. Not surprisingly, in situations like that, unlikely bonds of affection were forged. One family we knew decided to keep a duck, and filled their Anderson shelter with water so that it would have somewhere to swim. They got fond of it, and when Xmas came decided not to kill it after all.

★ ★ ★

Lamb Street recovered to some extent after the bombing. About half of the houses were made habitable again, the rest demolished and replaced by asbestos prefabs. No. 51 was repaired by the Corporation: but by then we were settled in the Hafod, and there was no question of our going back. My Mother took me over to Lamb Street, after the house had been repaired, to get some things we had left in the garden. How odd it was to go into the kitchen, with the familiar black-leaded grate, and find a family of strangers sitting at the table.

Two

Life in the Hafod

My Gran's house in Aberdyberthi Street in the Hafod was a small, working class dwelling, two up and three down, much like our house in Lamb Street, but Gran was living there alone. My Uncle Jack used to live with her, but he was eighteen when the War started and had just been called up for service in the Air Force.

"There's room for all of us at Gran's," my Mother told me after the Lamb Street bombing. "Years ago, when I was small, fourteen people could be living in that house, our relatives used to come down from Mountain Ash for their holiday."

"How did they all manage to sleep, then?"

"In the beds, of course. Spoon fashion, to save room. And Gran used to make chips like buggery."

The Hafod was only a mile or so distant from Waun Wen, had any crow wished to fly the distance, but for me it was an entirely different world. Lamb Street was not very interesting, from a boy's point of view: it was bounded at one end by the brown sandstone wall of Cwmfelin, and there was little to be seen from our back bedroom window except a few bedraggled gardens. The Hafod, on the other hand, lay directly under the vast, grey expanse of Kilvey Hill, long since poisoned by ancient lead works; Neath Road, the main thoroughfare to London and the valleys ran through it, and beyond that there was open access to railway lines, a disused canal and the River Tawe, at that point still tidal and muddy. People in one or two houses could even glimpse Swansea Bay.

Social life in the Hafod was quite different, too. In Lamb Street, as I have mentioned, my Mother kept very much to herself, and hardly anyone ventured into our house. Gran, on the other hand, was a welcoming soul, very much one of the crowd, and her house was a recognised port of call for family and neighbours. Our front door was always open and people were dropping to see 'Auntie Edie' all the time.

The stone back-kitchen at No. 64 was an improvement on the wooden lean-to we had in Lamb Street, but the house had its own problems. Every room was packed with furniture, for nothing was ever thrown out. Apart from that, Gran was almost paralysed from the waist down, and needed things to hold on to as she tottered around. She had not been upstairs for years. Her main pillars of support in the kitchen were the table, covered with sticky oilcloth, a little oak writing desk, and the mahogany sewing machine, which years before had provided the main family income. She also clung to the backs of some sagging Edwardian chairs whose springs pressed precariously against the worn plush covers.

The room was dominated by the fireplace – cleaning it, black-leading it, and lighting the fire took Gran the best part of an hour every morning. Like everyone else in the street, we were always carrying shovelfuls of coal, brushing up grit, and washing our hands after. In the summer, however, we moved to the back kitchen, where the grate was smaller, and was not always lit. There was, of course, no running water inside the house – our tap, like everybody else's, was out in the back yard. The lav was distant, down the garden. Much of the moisture in the house was unwanted, coming from a leak in the roof and rising damp. The wallpaper in the back kitchen, for instance, hung loose like a flag, and I was always afraid to touch it lest it come away altogether. By the time we moved in from Lamb Street the Corporation had provided electricity, though one gas mantle had been left in the parlour. The "electric" was a great step forward, and saved (among other things) mucking about with glass batteries for the wireless. But we only had a simple light-ing circuit, and our few appliances – the small stained electric fire and my Mother's iron – had to be connected to the bulb sockets which hung from the ceiling. I seemed to be for ever climbing on chairs and stretching up. The problem was partly solved one day when the iron blew up, and my Mother, unnerved, went back to the cast-iron ones you warmed on the fire.

The house was a shivery place to live in, especially in winter-time. The narrow stair went straight up from the kitchen, so drafts from the bedrooms swept down into the living area, scarcely impeded by the ill-fitting bedroom doors. Despite roaring fires we lived in a swirl of cold air. There was only one warm corner, the one nearest the fireplace, and that is where Gran passed her evenings, stolidly ignoring the complaints directed against her occupancy. Heating the bedrooms was out of the question, and we never used sheets: woollen blankets seemed to warm you up quicker. So at night, I would fall asleep in a cosy, rough cocoon. If I were in the back bedroom, I would be lulled by the clanking and snorting of the engines in the shunting yard down Maliphant Street.

The Hafod may have been a different world, but many of the things I liked were the same, especially the food.

"You're a growing boy," my Mother would say, putting an enormous plateful of something in front of me. "You've got to eat well!"

Although she could not clean much, Gran managed to keep on cooking, and my Mother enjoyed it as well. They both did as much as possible on the kitchen fire, in soot-encrusted saucepans, to save money on gas, but we also had a blackened and long since uncleanable gas stove. Usually I sat down to four cooked meals a day – breakfast, dinner, a cooked tea, and a hefty supper (about ten o'clock). I came to love a lot of the 'austerity', war-time food – corned beef and spam with boiled potatoes, suet pudding, tripe simmered with onions. There was the impressive fry-up of cockles, laverbread, bacon and sausages on Saturdays, when the cockle-women came around: there hadn't been any in Lamb Street. War or not, a Sunday roast was never missed, with roast and boiled potatoes, two veg., and fresh tart to follow. "Some people haves their Sunday dinner without the meat," my Mother said, "if they can't get it." But we never reached that sorry state. On the other hand, fresh fruit and salad were despised – a fact which was to have unexpected consequences for me later on.

"It's hot today," my Mother might say on a summer's day. "I think we'll have nice salad with salt, pepper and vinegar." My heart would sink. We all drank pints of strong tea at all hours – in fact, if it were not almost black Gran would not touch it.

* * *

I could not write about the years I spent in the Hafod without saying a good deal about my maternal Grandmother. Looking back over my boyhood, I think she was the person I loved most: a small, plump woman with short grey hair, a round face, and kindly eyes, she was the epitome of patience and goodness. (My affection for my Mother, as I shall relate, eventually came to be tinged with resentment.)

I never heard Gran utter a spiteful word about a living soul – her greatest vice was the consumption of the occasional half-pint of beer. Wholesome food, warm clothes regardless of fashion, and tidiness about the house were part of her nature. Naturally, she had her little idiosyncrasies. She hated change of any kind, and adamantly refused to wear her false teeth, which irritated my Mother greatly.

"Why can't you keep a set of teeth in your 'ead?" my Mother, an acerbic creature if there was one, shouted one day, when Gran was trying to eat an apple by scraping it with a spoon as best she could. My Mother's own habit of keeping her dentures, of which she had a partial set, on the mantelpiece never struck her as odd, even when they had bits of toffee sticking to them.

Gran's life had been a series of tragedies, which were related to me bit by bit, as time went by. In 1909, her husband Iono, who was in his early thirties, developed appendicitis.

"I was afraid for him to go into hospital," Gran told me, "so I decided to look after him myself in the front bedroom. But the appendix broke and poisoned him. We called the doctor, and he tried to operate on him in bed, but it was too late. I wore his cap." (Which was the custom of the day.)

My Grandfather left Gran penniless with five children to support. She did, however, have an unmarried sister (my great aunt Sal) and her younger brother Joe to help. The women scraped a living by sewing clothes on the old treadle sewing machine ("Sixpence for an apron," said Gran, "but we had to use our own cotton"). Joe, however, died of an illness in 1911, at the age of twenty six.

The youngest of the children, a little boy also called Joe, had meningitis.

"He was very sensitive about his large head," my Mother told me later. "Gran made a big cap to fit him. He was a lovely little boy. But he had a problem balancing himself. When he walked, he could only keep upright by touching the walls and furniture and things. Light as a fairy, though. He died when he was eight. We all loved him."

Gran did not have much interest in education, but she did her best for the children who survived. Hard work at the sewing machine allowed her to give my Uncle Gilbert an apprenticeship as a plumber and some music lessons. My mother, the cleverest of the three daughters, somehow got to a secondary school, as I have related. My Auntie Annie learned to be a tailoress, but Auntie Olive (who was certainly the least able) went to work in Lewis Lewis's, the drapers. My great Auntie Sal developed cancer while still in her early fifties, and died in 1930. All of this was known to me, but one other dark, dark tragedy of those days was carefully concealed. It will find a place later in these pages.

All four surviving children, including my mother, got married, but more trouble was to come. Soon after the outbreak of war, when we were still in Lamb Street, my Uncle Gilbert died. He was only forty two, living with his wife (my Auntie Kate) and their two children lower down Aberdyberthi Street. Gilbert was a big man, and rough in appearance, but he would sit at the piano in the parlour for hours, a cigarette hanging from his lip, his cap pushed back over his balding head, playing with consummate skill. I can also remember him sucking water out of a lead pipe, in preparation for a soldering job. Perhaps that is why he developed cancer of the lung (which my Mother always delicately referred to as a 'tumour').

The final blow was all too familiar to me – Gran's paralysis, which I had to live with every day. Eventually I got a story from my Mother, though it may not have been accurate.

"One day Gran felt giddy in the street, when she was coming back with some shopping. She fell and hit her head on the pavement. She didn't faint, but soon after she felt a creeping numbness in her legs. It got worse and worse."

"Didn't she go and see a doctor, Ma?" I asked.

"Well, she didn't have much money, and they didn't think about doctors in those days. It came on bit by bit, see."

By the time we moved in to No. 64 Gran had difficulty in getting around even in the house, and her bed had to be moved downstairs to the front parlour, where the piano was. She would, of an evening, ask me to give her my arm and help her to bed. (I was always annoyed, though, if she asked me just when I was sitting down to supper). In the mornings she found she could only get some feeling into her legs by stamping them on the floor for five or ten minutes, so the bumps became a regular part of the household noise. She could not bend over, and one of my minor duties, every month or so, was to wash her feet and cut her toenails.

As the paralysis got worse, so did Gran's virtually unmentionable problem: we had no lavatory or washing facilities in the house, and she had to manage with a bucket in the yard. She did her best to keep herself clean, but at times the smell from her poor unwashed body was too embarrassing to talk about. I was always afraid that the one or two friends I had would come in and notice it. Indeed, as time went by her falls, and the lack of any facilities for looking after her, turned life into a nightmare: and Gran herself suffered most.

One day I came home from school to find her lying on the kitchen floor, in tears, while my Auntie Enid, who lived just up the street, looked on helplessly.

"Good job I came in," she said, almost in tears herself. "She fell down when she was trying to reach the potatoes. I can't get her up by myself, she's too heavy."

The two of us together managed to lift her onto a chair, so that she could at least get on with the cooking. A wheel-chair was out of the question – they were big, clumsy things, too big for us, and too expensive for us to buy, anyway. So Gran sat there, day after day, in her tiny confined world, unable even to go out into the street where she had always lived.

* * *

The bombing of Lamb Street and our hurried arrival meant that Gran had to accommodate a family of three, with pieces of furniture for which there was hardly any room. On top of all that, she did not like my Father.

It was, I believe, living with Gran that caused another break-up of my parents' marriage. Conditions in No. 64 were too difficult for my fastidious father – a small house without hot water, nowhere to wash in private, a mother-in-law who was crippled, toothless, and as he saw it socially inferior. The two worlds, Matthews's and Jones's, just did not fit. When my Father sat at the kitchen table I could feel the tension. He was further put off by the Jones's complete ignorance of social proprieties and occasional bad language (words like 'bugger', 'bloody' and 'cowing' – whatever that meant – were frequent). Gran, despite her mild disposition, started finding fault with William Alfred, and even developed a graphic description, for the benefit of neighbours, of how wastefully he ate pork chops. He disregarded all the fat, which Gran had eaten all her life.

Jack's home-coming on a few days' leave did not help, either. Small and unobtrusive, Jack did not seem to take up much room, or cause any bother. But he had received some education (he had matriculated at Dynevor Secondary School), and had worked briefly in the office of Hancocks' brewery. He certainly had nothing in common with my Father, who seemed embarrassed by his presence. In fact, the two hardly spoke.

Be that as it may, one sunny morning in June 1941, after the umpteenth quarrel, my Father decided that life in the Hafod was no longer tolerable, especially as he had a larger house with hot water, a table-topped bath, and a doting mother awaiting him in St. Thomas. He went upstairs, threw a few things into his suitcase, and brought it down. He paused in the narrow passage which led from the kitchen to the front door, and turned to me.

"Come on Son," he said, "we'll go over to Gamma's!"

The proposal provoked cries of outrage from my Mother and Gran.

"Oh, he's not going!" my Mother shouted as she grabbed me and pulled me back into the kitchen. "He's mine! Aren't you, Mervyn?" (My Mother, for some reason always called me Mervyn, and my Father 'Son'.)

"No, he's not," said Dad. "He's mine. Come with me, Son!" He gave his usual, slightly twisted smile.

But I was greatly puzzled: did I 'belong' to my Mother or to my Father? Had I but known it, this was one of the great turning points in my life. Deep down, however, my ties with my Mother were binding absolutely. I could not possibly leave her. I looked in silence as my Mother clutched me.

My Father was insistent, and the row dragged on, each side claiming me for its own. Eventually my Father went off, leaving me in the hands of the Hafod faction. All this time the front door was wide open, and Marge Stanbury, the Catholic woman who lived opposite, was watching developments intently from her front window sill, where she seemed to spend most of her life. Such rich material for gossip was not to be missed.

After my Father left tensions eased, and (as I was on my Mother's side) I hardly felt upset at all. I think Gran was relieved, too, but I could not divine my Mother's feelings, behind the blaze of anger, that is. I was certainly pleased by the prospect of less authority. My Father had never devoted much time or attention to me, and he could be quite restrictive. Unlike my Mother's side of the family, he disliked cats, so now we would be able to have one. In the event we acquired a little tortoiseshell stray, a she called Poly, who would sit on her hind legs and beg. She was the only cat I ever knew that could do that. My Father had managed to salvage the tool shed from Lamb Street, and set it up in the garden of No. 64, so I got that and all his tools as part of the bargain. They were well worth having.

* * *

My Mother was so different from Gran that an outsider might have found it hard to believe that they were mother and daughter. Whereas Gran had always been (to judge from an early photograph) plump and relaxed, my Mother was petite, nervy, and not all that easy to get on with. Gran was not very clever and rarely showed any sign of wanting to do anything in particular, but my

Mother possessed an intense desire to get on in life. After my Father departed relations between the two women began to deteriorate: and looking back, I think this was as much due to differences in temperament as to my Mother's resentment over the collapse of her marriage and the need to live with an elderly cripple.

With Gran in such a sad state, my Mother's dominance in the house grew apace, and I became increasingly aware of her foibles, not least her ineptitude at housework. My visits to other boys' homes made me ever more aware of the grime and lack of order in ours. "I know I'm not very good at housework," she would declare. "I've never liked it, really." Under my Mother's management, and Gran's despairing gaze, our modest dwelling would reach its most chaotic state on Sunday mornings. Mother would begin by cooking her breakfast, usually a couple of pieces of bacon, in a chipped enamel saucer, which also served as a breakfast plate.

Then, leaving some of the breakfast things, including the milk bottle and the heavily encrusted sugar bowl, on the table, she would partly wash the dishes; half black-lead the grate (if Gran had not done it) and light the fire; start, but not finish, a bit of laundry, which was boiled on a Primus stove in the back yard, to save gas; clean some, but not all of the vegetables for lunch; perhaps put the meat in the oven; feed the cat; and fit in a little desultory dusting. On wet days the fire might not catch straight away, and have to be started several times over, filling the kitchen with acrid smoke; "There's a smeech!" my Mother would declare. By the end of the morning even I could see that she did not know whether she was coming or going.

This ineptitude was aggravated by a genuine inability to recognise honest dirt. The dishes and saucepans were never washed properly, the carpet on the flagged kitchen floor was always gritty with coal dust, and the idea of cleaning out a cupboard, or washing behind a piece of furniture, was utterly foreign to her. Her passion for hoarding meant that all nooks and crannies filled with empty jars, tins, newspapers, bags, dusters, rags and anything that might conceivably, one day, be useful. In fact I started doing the same thing myself, until it turned into a life-long habit.

"Ma," I would say, despairingly, "can't you keep things a bit cleaner? You put this cup back in the cupboard dirty."

She would look at it and literally see nothing amiss.

"There's nothing wrong with that," she would say resentfully. "Why don't you help me a bit more? If you did we could turn this house into a little palace." She would turn her palms outward as though presenting me with an invisible gift.

Set against all of this were certain clear virtues. Unlike my Father, she was a very truthful person, and passed on to me a horror of lies. She was deeply concerned about my welfare, and would never allow me to leave the house inadequately clothed or shod. She took a keen interest in my health, which was to pay dividends, and evinced a constant concern about my progress at school.

Her musical talent was undoubted. We had no piano in Lamb Street, but at Gran's my Mother could play the great ebony instrument in the parlour, and like Uncle Gilbert fill the whole house with melody. I greatly envied her ability to do so. Musicality was in the family, and her father, though lacking half a finger, considered himself to be a semi-professional.

"I never had any lessons, mind," she told me. "Gran just couldn't afford them."

"How did you learn, then?"

"Your Uncle Gilbert used to have lessons," she replied, "and when he came home I would try and copy him. But you can have lessons if you want to. There's a teacher over in Waun Wen who does them for five shillings an hour."

"I'd like that," I said.

And indeed I tried dutifully for a few weeks. Alas, I did not take to them, and in my Mother's absence (she was out working most of the time) I failed to keep practising. The result was that despite my fondness for music I never gained mastery of an instrument.

My Mother had some arithmetical skills also. She got on quite well as a comptometer operator (it was a simple adding and subtracting machine used in accounts) and could help me with my homework. She told me she had been a very sensitive child. Gran, in great need of extra coppers, made her work as a baby-sitter for nine pence a week when she was only a child herself; my Mother had been ashamed when obliged to help on a vegetable stall in Swansea Market, and feared that girls from her school might see her. Had she been born in different circumstances, she would, I am sure, have been no stranger to the concert platform. And bounded though her horizons were, she knew it.

* * *

The departure of my Father, and my Mother's lack of domesticity meant that there was no one to do repairs and odd jobs around the house. The only handyman in sight was Mr. Crocker from Neath

Road. He was in the enlistment age-group, but had not been called up because he only had one hand. This did not improve his work skills, nor (alas) moderate his prices. So on attaining the robust age of ten or so I decided I could do things better myself – and for nothing.

Painting was the first thing I turned my hand to, if only because my Mother's mentality seemed to lack the concept of a straight edge. Soon I was messing about with the tins of undrying buff and stumpy brushes which my Father had left behind. Next I moved on to making, or at least trying to make, a tool cupboard from an orange-box. The wood came from the greengrocer's, while the nails and screws were bought by the ounce in Woolworth's. (I found that if you joked with the girls there they gave you more). The finished item, however, was not successful, mainly because it had a curtain instead of a door.

"Oh, Ma," I said, peering into it one day. "The cat must have gone in and peed all over my tools. They're all rusty!"

"Oh, Gawd!" she replied. "There's awful!"

One job I refused to do was wallpapering, which I regarded as sissy; but as time went by I attempted small improvements in our primitive electric system – a new socket here, a switch there. Experience of electric shocks soon followed, but mercifully I avoided electrocution. My friend John Lewis warned me about it. One day, he said, he had donned an old pair of ear-phones, and stuck the wires in an electric socket, to see what you could hear. His father told him afterwards that he was only saved by the thickness of the bakelite. Gran always objected to my electrical activities, and adamantly refused to let me fix up a lamp near her bed in the parlour. She preferred to manage with a candle in an old enamel holder which she would balance on a wobbly aspidistra stand. By some miracle, it never got knocked over.

* * *

My Grandmother's kindness and her interest in what was happening roundabout meant that relatives and neighbours were always running in for a gossip. One of the most frequent visitors was my Auntie Mary, or Meiry, as we pronounced it, Auntie Enid's Mother. She was Gran's sister-in-law, having been married to my great Uncle Mog, and she shared Gran's taste for half a pint of mild. A small, grey-haired woman, she would slip in through the passage almost unnoticed.

"Have you got nine pence for a glass, Edie?" she would ask. "Mild or bitter? I'll just slip down to the Smiths to get it."

She would return half and hour later and take up a strategic position at the kitchen table, vastly complicating anything I was doing on it. I chafed at her ability to make the glass last so long. Would she never go? One day she came in when my Mother was washing her hair with a lotion that gave off an appalling stench.

"Nasty smell, isn't it?" she said. "I never washes my hair, myself, mind." I looked at her grey locks curiously, wondering whether there was anything living in them.

Auntie Mary had three grown daughters, Enid, Florry and Doris, who all lived within a couple of hundred yards of us. Her youngest grandchildren, my cousins Donny, Gordon and Jackie, were a source of constant concern.

"I worries about them boys," she would say. "Our Gordon didn' come back from the sands [Swansea beach] yesterday, and I went all the way down to look for 'im... 'Aven't our Jackie got a beautiful 'ead of 'air?" As far as I could see it was perfectly normal. For some reason she took less interest in Donny, my Auntie Enid's son, a handsome little boy with a dimple on his cheek. He was two years younger than I but my closest friend in the family.

Of all the people who came to our house, perhaps the most wonderful was Enid, who lived with Auntie Mary in No. 58. She had a round face, rather like Gran's, with an unvarying kindly expression. Her main tasks in life were looking after Donny, her mother, her husband (whom she always referred to by his full name – Jack Thomas). Since Jack Thomas was out of work as often as he was in it, and only a labourer at that, their household was one of the poorest in the street. They had gas mantles long after everyone else had gone over to electricity, and I remember my Mother saying, one Christmas: "There's awful, isn't it, Enid could only manage a one-and-six rabbit for their Christmas dinner this year."

Enid knew no life other than what went on immediately around her, but like Gran seemed perfectly satisfied with her lot. She called in to see everyone several times a day, and did bits of shopping for anyone who could not get out. She also spent a lot of time on her doorstep (like Marge Stanbury) watching people passing, and calling out to those she knew ("Maisie, have the milkman been yet? Or the bread?") It was Enid who came to our house every day, faithful and unpaid, to empty Gran's endless slops, run errands (or 'messages', as we called them), and keep us up to date on the news.

I was always surprised by her meek obedience to Jack Thomas, perhaps because he kept her, and she knew that if she didn't do what he said, he'd give her a good wallop. So although their family was by no means quiet (they squabbled from time to time) the atmosphere was healthy, and there was none of the bitterness which permeated ours. Jack Thomas couldn't spend much money on drink because he didn't have any: and Enid had a way of taking even the worst disasters with a smile. I remember her coming in once after Donny had started smoking, and burnt a hole in his new suit.

"I asked him how he done it," she said, "and he told me he must have put a meg back in his pocket when it was still alight. He said it was cigarette ash. Cigabloodyrette ash, indeed!"

"Our Donny," she said on another occasion, "have broken the alarm clock. It's terrible. We haven't got a bit of time in the house."

How often I wished that my Mother, Lily Jones had been blessed with the same equanimity.

Another neighbour Gran saw a lot of was Florry Luxton, who lived opposite. Mrs. Luxton had one of the polestone-fronted houses with three bedrooms and a bathroom, but (fair play) she never allowed this to spoil her social relations. Small, stooping and with thick glasses, she was devoted to godliness (as interpreted at Mount Pleasant Chapel), her daughter Maisie, who was a district nurse, and a variety of domestic pets. We took care not to utter any swear-words when she came over. She was a good-natured old woman, but she usually came with her revolting fat spaniel Della, which we all hated. It learned to scramble onto one of our Edwardian chairs and open our loose-fitting cupboard door with its snout. There was always a flurry of 'Shoo's' and 'get down's', and "She'll have the sponge" when Della was there. Fortunately, Florry left her dreadfully overfed cats at home, though she kept us up to date on their various activities.

Gran had another relative of her own generation, her half-sister Hannah, who lived up in Gerald Street. Auntie Hannah was one of the two members of our family who was actually illiterate. (The other was my Auntie Mary Lizzy who did not go to school because she had St. Vitus's Dance — whatever that was — and twitched her whole life through.) Auntie Hannah had apparently been orphaned as a child, and handed over to a mysterious Auntie Jane who wouldn't let the little girl go to school, because it was too cruel.

Auntie Hannah was a large, morose woman with a strange repu-tation for breaking things. I remember being sent up on an errand one evening and finding their kitchen lit by a candle. The flames cast long, unsteady shadows on the walls.

"They've cut off the electric," Auntie Hannah announced. "You haven't got an oil lamp down there we could borrow for a few days, have you?"

Since everyone was using them in the air-raid shelters, it was hard to deny that we had one.

"I'll find out, Auntie Hannah," I said.

Shortly after, I took one up, and returned to collect it a few days later.

Auntie Hannah gave me a dark, lugubrious look.

"I'm sorry, son," she said, "the globe got smashed, see. But I managed to get another, it isn't quite the right size, but you can still use it, can't you?"

The glass shades were not easy to get, and I found that the replacement would only fit if you put it on the burner upside down... Another strange thing about Auntie Hannah was that she hardly ever came to see Gran, though there were no ill feelings between them.

"I don't know why Hannah never comes down," Gran would say. "I haven't seen her for years."

Next door up, in number 63, lived Mrs. Sal Jones and her husband Tom. Sal was another of those neat, aproned women, a bit like Gamma over in Osterley Street, who kept everything spick and span. Sal, it is true, did not come in very often, but Gran, one evening a week, until her legs failed completely, would struggle into Mrs. Jones' for a glass of beer. The two ladies had lived next door to one another since the twenties, but never called one another anything but 'Mrs. Jones' and 'Mrs. Jones'. Sal's husband, Tom, was a hale and hearty railwayman, already in sight of retirement when we moved to No. 64. Her two sons had secure jobs, (Tom drove a taxi, and Jackie was also 'on the line'). All four daughters – Queeny, Addy, Peggy, and Kitty – made comfortable marriages devoid, it would seem, of clubs, pubs, and boozing, and came home every Wednesday to clean the house, which (unlike ours) always smelt fresh and pleasant, with a spicing of Tom's tobacco.

Sal Jones and her brood formed a sort of next-door ideal which we could never match – they were happy, united, and seemed to have avoided all real trouble – at least there was none of the tragedy which had troubled our household. I only heard of Sal having one row ever, and that was caused by Tom Jones's well-known parsimony. She had filched some money from his money box and put buttons in instead, so that it would still rattle. He played hell when he found out.

Almost opposite us, in another of the pole-stone houses, lived Miss Elsie Morris, the credit draper. The 'Miss' was important because she had been trying to get married for as long as anyone could remember. Aged about forty when we moved in, she earned a living by buying selections of clothes from local warehouses and selling them to poor families on a weekly payment basis. Her shop was in the front parlour, and her bargains hung in the window. She was eternally out collecting money.

Everybody knew she had a double hernia, but this did not stop her commercial activities. My Mother, despite her rheumatic feet, took a critical interest in Elsie's gait, and would sometimes comment on it.

"I saw Elsie Morris struggling up Monger Street this morning," she would say expressively, "Gawd, I don't know how she manages to put... one... leg in front of the other."

Elsie played a small but important role in my life. She brought me into contact with her nephew, John Lewis who lived in Mayhill, but came down to stay in their house from time to time. He was a couple of years older than I, but he was bright, active, and I admired him immensely. He soon became my best friend – my only friend in the Hafod, really, since I did not bother much with my cousins or my classmates in school. John always seemed to be ready to do interesting things, like going to see good pictures, collecting stamps, keeping a rabbit, and also a duck in their flooded Anderson shelter. Mercifully, he had little interest in sport. I enjoyed his company so much that when the time came for him to go home, up Mayhill, I would walk all the way with him. Then he would walk part of the way back with me... It was called 'sending'. We spent many evenings together.

Elsie also showed me my first corpse. When her mother died, Elsie had her laid out for viewing in the middle room. The neighbours drew their curtains, as usual, as a sign of mourning. If you happened to be passing and Elsie saw you, she would invite you in to see it. One day she caught me.

"Would you like to see John's Gran before she's buried?" she said.

A dead body? I thought. Of course I would. "Oh, yes Auntie Elsie!"

She led me in, but I paused at the threshold of the darkened room, rather frightened.

"Go on," said Elsie, "go in and have a proper look."

Her mother (John's Gran) had been dressed in a sort of frilly white nightshirt, and was lying in an open coffin. The thought that the old woman was dead was the only awe-inspiring thing about it, for there was nothing really unpleasant about the pale, silent face. For some reason the old lady's hand lay across the edge of the polished wood: I touched one of the bony fingers, while Elsie looked on approvingly. It was a marvellous thing to tell people afterwards. Then Elsie said one other thing which somehow stuck in my mind.

"Pity your brother isn't home, he could see it too."

"Brother?" I said, "I haven't got a brother. You mean my Uncle Jack?" How could she make such a mistake, I thought, living just opposite.

By far the worst family in the street were Llew and Annie and their brood consisting (I seem to recall) of four children. Llew was an unobtrusive little man with thick glasses, no aim in life, and no job to go with it. He would creep down to the pub, wearing an old blue suit, minding his own business. His wife was jolly, overweight, ginger-haired, dishevelled, and a good fighter. Their Saturday night rows, when they were both drunk, were proverbial, and their way of life was regarded as a prime example of how Hafod people should not behave. Their house was noted for its long ignored water leaks and general air of desolation. Their three younger children were a tough lot, too, while the oldest boy, Evan, already in his teens, was evidently destined to follow in his father's footsteps. We saw them nearly every day, but I don't think any of them ever crossed our threshold.

I was particularly afraid of the second daughter, who was several years older than I and, I always thought, a nasty piece of work. We exchanged insults on many occasions.

"Ha, ha!" I would shout, with a grimace. "All your father and mother does is drink."

"And all your Mother does is play the bloody piano!"

One of the irritating things about Llew and Annie's younger offspring was their practice of attending Sunday school the week before the annual picnic, so that they could take part. (My Sunday School attendance, as boring as ever, had continued in the Aberdyberthi Street mission hall.) Needless to say, they would not be seen there again until the following year. The rest of us had to put up with it for the whole twelve months.

Occasionally, we had callers whom we did not know. We heated water for washing clothes in large tin 'boilers' on a Primus stove out the back, paraffin being much cheaper than gas. However, you could only get the boilers from the gypsy women who came around selling them. These strange folk would suddenly appear at the door, hung round with their bulky wares, and demand that you bought one.

I shall never forget the day a large, self-assured female pushed her way in to our passage. "Can I come in for a minute, love?" she said, unstoppable. She went straight through to the back kitchen where Gran was cooking the dinner, and plonked herself down in the corner. Sensing, perhaps, Gran's kind and yielding nature, she refused to budge until we had bought a boiler and given her a meal. Then, casting a knowing eye around the room, she rattled off a list of items which she thought we might like to give her. Clearly, she had considerable experience of the situation. My Mother was at work, and Gran and I got more and more apprehensive as the hours went by. Eventually, the gypsy took up her boilers and condescended to leave, with nothing more than a full stomach. We made damn sure that no one like that ever came in again.

The Catholic nuns were gentler, but hardly less unnerving. I think it was their garb, and the knowledge that they had taken things called 'vows' that did it. There would be a knock on the door at some totally unexpected hour, perhaps late afternoon. You opened it to find a hooded, black-robed figure on the step, her face sort of hemmed in by a white starched band. She would probably be collecting for the Dr. Barnardo's Orphanage on Fairwood Common, so there was no question of refusing. I would run into the kitchen for a thrupenny or sixpenny bit, return as quickly as possible, and drop it into a small clean hand. An Irish voice would say 'God bless you', and the nun, with a swish of her mysterious robes, would move on to the next house.

★ ★ ★

The Hafod at that time was very much a self-contained community with a great variety of shops, some of them, like Elsie's, in the front parlour. The pawnbroker's with its three golden balls was still functioning; there were two fish and chip shops with coal-fired frying ranges, two butchers, several grocers, greengrocers, a chemist's. There was a combined post-office and optician's, and a garage. Three pubs did a good business, though we kept out of them.

Since everybody loved meat (no vegetarian nonsense in those days) and meat was scarce, the butchers wielded tremendous influence. They were widely suspected of 'doing well' out of the war, and the cuts they sold were a daily topic of conversation among the women. Once the butcher at the top of Neath Road, desperate for something to sell, devised new sausages. He was in fact Jack Thomas's brother, and Auntie Enid 'registered' with him in the hope of doing a bit better. One day she ran in to tell us the horrible tale of their frying.

"When I turned up the gas," she said, "they all fell to pieces, they was only skin, fat, and breadcrumbs. Oh, Jesus, I was ashamed to put them on Jack Thomas's plate."

Of course, none of the women dared complain, for fear of doing even worse. Our own butcher, Bryn Thomas, was always full of smiles, and said "Much obliged" after every sale; but whether his good humour derived from a happy disposition or a full till, no one knew.

We used to buy some groceries from a shop called Davey's down on Neath Road. It was run by a tiny, bespectacled spinster called Dorothy. When you went in she would glide, ghost-like, through the gloomy premises – the window was cluttered and she begrudged using the electric. One day I went in to get a bottle of coffee essence, the kind with a colourful turbaned prince on the label, which everyone in the Hafod bought if they liked coffee. As Dorothy was serving me an immensely tall, but bowed lady came in, the one who was known to be 'not all there'. She was carrying a cup and saucer with a brown liquid in it.

"Dorothy," she whispered (she always whispered) "I bought this coffee here and I'm bringing it back for you to taste. It tastes like cardboard, in deed to Gawd! Go on, 'ave some, try it."

"I'm too busy serving this boy."

Dorothy finished doing so, and I went off, wondering how the drama would develop. I'd never eaten cardboard, but you could sort of guess what it tasted like.

The social pinnacle of the Neath Road trade was occupied, arguably, by Mr. Gardener, the local chemist and expert in therapeutics. You went to see him if you couldn't afford to see the doctor, which was usually the case. The incidence of physical disorder was high, so Mr. Gardener always had people coming in for consultations. I felt thoroughly ill at ease in his shop, it was all so spotless, expensive and smelt of disinfectant. A couple of snooty girls in white coats would emerge from the dispensary at the back and ask what you wanted. If necessary, they would call him out, small, trim and bespectacled, to tell you what to buy. Eventually, he took to drink, which sometimes led to confusion in his prescriptions.

"You got to be careful with Gardener now," Enid told us one day (she knew everything). "Last week he gave Florry George the wrong medicine and nearly killed her. Her daughter went down to complain."

At the other end of the social scale was Mr. Kramsky, thought to be Russian, and the main 'rag and bone' merchant in the Hafod. In fact he specialised in scrap metal and every boy in the Hafod knew his great yard down the Strand. Anything that was the least bit rickety would be derided as having come from there.

"Where did you get your bony-shaker then, been down Kramsky's, 'ave you?"

Jack Kramsky, dour and red-faced, clad invariably in a dark blue suit, would sit day after day in a booth at the entrance to his domain, apparently oblivious to the stench of dirt and rusting metal which it exuded. He would argue endlessly over the loads of scrap that the rag-and-bone men brought in on their carts. His business, I imagine, throve greatly from the war munitions drive, and behind the scenes he may have been quite well off.

One day I slipped into his yard partly out of curiosity, partly in the hope of finding some old tools. He took no notice of me whatever because he was dealing with a couple of young men who had just dumped their scrap on his weigh-bridge scale, which was set in the earthen floor. Their horse clinked its hooves restlessly outside as Kramsky slid the weight deftly along the gradations on the bar. "A hundredweight," he declared, and reached for his wallet.

"No, it's not," said one of the men. "I saw the bar. It was well over."

Mr. K's English wasn't very good, but he swore with great fluency. "Oh, f—king hell," he said. "Jesus Christ. No it wasn't. The bloody weights and measures inspector was here, see. He couldn't get over it. The wind blows under them soding scales and makes the weight look more than it is. Honest to Gawd! But I'll keep my word, I'll give you what I said" (which was, of course, less than they wanted).*

---

*As it happened, Kramsky was later linked to one of the Hafod's greatest disasters. Some fifty feet above his scrap yard, on the same level as Prince of Wales Road, was a row of old red-brick houses which he owned and let, mostly to poor Jews from East Europe. (Among them was a sinister man in a skull cap who twice chased me along the street when I stared at him; and a fat man who spoke with such a thick accent that even the bus conductors could not understand him when he told them where he wanted to get off.) Anyway, the high foundations of the houses were probably rat-infested and unsafe. But Kramsky hoped to sell them, nevertheless, and

★ ★ ★

Unlike Waun Wen, the Hafod was hardly affected by the bombing, but there was a dramatic instance of belligerence at Greco's Café down on Neath Road. One morning Enid rushed in with the news.

"The police have been and arrested Greco," she exclaimed. "There's a big commotion in the street."

The café was run by Mr Greco himself, a small, dark-haired Italian. Apart from the few words needed for his business, he spoke little English: but his attractive black-haired daughters, who helped him around the tea urn, were born and bred in the Hafod, and everybody knew them. Behind the shop was a little glass-roofed pavilion with tables and curved plywood seats where you could enjoy a cup of tea and an Eynon's pie while watching the girls serve the customers. When Italy entered the war the establishment must have come under suspicion – either because there was some sort of instruction covering all Italians, or because the police thought Greco was a spy.

Whatever the reason, such an exciting event was not to be missed. I rushed down to Neath Road and found an excited crowd outside the café. Somebody had already smashed Greco's window for him, and his family had retreated upstairs, in anticipation of a siege. There was a poignant moment when one of the girls, her dark eyes blazing, leaned out of the bedroom window to address the crowd. Everyone looked up in anticipation.

"My Father isn't a spy," she yelled, in the broadest of Hafod accents. "He lived in the Hafod with you for thirty years. Go away, you Welsh swine!"

Then she disappeared behind the curtains. The crowd seemed to be more excited than angry, for nobody, I am sure, thought there was anything to fear from poor Greco. Later the shop window was boarded up, and although the cafe remained shut, life in that bit of Neath Road returned to normal, with Beale's shoe repairers and Bevan's fish and chip shop functioning as before. To finish the tale: Greco never reappeared at the counter, but one of his daughters married another Italian, and they kept the business going for several years.

---

one had a 'For Sale' notice in the window. Early one morning, in September, 1950 when the occupants were still abed, the whole row collapsed into the gulf below, and many sleepers never woke to see the light of dawn. Strangely enough the continuous facade was left standing at pavement level, with the notice still hanging eerily in the window aperture.

My main outdoor pleasure, after I got to the Hafod, was watching steam locomotives. Looking back, I cannot explain this interest, nor trace it to any particular event. I had, of course, been fascinated enough by moving pistons to ask for a steam engine as a Christmas present when we were living in Lamb Street. *The Thrilling Book for Boys* which Auntie Olive gave me contained an account of how steam engines worked, with a simple diagram. Thus I acquired (or so I thought) the key to a true understanding of 'reciprocating' machinery – with pistons and valves – throughout the world. Things which just span, like the Reverend Parson's steam turbine, dynamos, electric motors, etc., were much less satisfying. Petrol and diesel engines which functioned by means of explosions in their cylinders were positively abhorrent. I longed to make a steam engine myself, but it was impossible. In the absence of a lathe I could only finger bits of copper tubing and canisters which might, if filed and soldered, serve as piston cylinders and boilers. I never managed it.

Behind Maliphant Street was a waste area adjoining the main line into High Street station and the Hafod sidings: if you climbed up the wall at the side you could get a close-up view of the engines as they clanked and fumed past. The wall had convenient footholds and was comfortable to sit on. Perched there, I must have watched dozens of engines go by, and inhaled an unbelievable amount of smoke and steam.

The excitement was unfailing. First, you listened for the distant rumble of wheels, and the dry pant of an exhaust. This would tell you whether to expect one of the big Kings or Castles, pulling a dozen long-distance coaches, or a smaller tank locomotive taking a stopping train down to Llanelly. The rumble would turn to a roar, the ground would tremble, and the monster was suddenly rolling past, its great wheels spinning with astounding ease. The sights and smells – everything to do with working locomotives – enthralled me. Sometimes I would try and persuade Donny Thomas to go with me. "Come down and watch the engines," I would say. "You'll see huge great driving wheels as big as your Father!" But neither Donny, nor anyone else, came more than once, so this pastime, too, was a solitary one. I wonder whether any of the engine crews ever noticed me on the wall as they went by.

There were other types of steam vehicle which could be enjoyed also. The fun fairs still had showmen's engines, all red paint and shining brass; there were steam rollers, the property of Swansea

Corporation, for levelling asphalt roads. I never really fathomed how they could reverse if they only had one cylinder – according to the *Thrilling Book for Boys*, this was a mechanical impossibility. Finally, a few antiquated steam lorries still chuffed their way up Prince of Wales Road, maintained in service for war-time needs. They sounded exactly like sewing machines, and dripped oil and hot water as they went. Inside the enormous cabs two blackened figures – a stoker and a driver – would work to keep them moving.

★　★　★

In 1942, at the age of nine and a half, I decided that all the interesting things happening to me should be set down on paper. Using a small cash book Uncle Jack had brought home from Wm. Hancock's Brewery Ltd., I began with a brief discourse on Roman castles, and followed it with a diary which I managed to keep going for a full three days, regardless of considerable spelling difficulties.

BRITON

Wales is a land ful of mountains. The roman's biult many castle's. There is Cardiff castle, Swansea, castle and Oystermouth castle. And a good many more. It is intruting to talk adout them. year's ago when the romans' lived there, it was a sight to watch them fire their arrowss'. I expect you have seen the crosse's and slits for them to fire their arrow's from the castle. In side the castles there are usaly bare. And you have to sleep on straw. and it is not very nice inside. by W.A.M. Matthew-s.

I have no idea why I used my Father's initials. But after a large number of sums, mostly wrong, I continued:

I am 9 years old My life Feb 19th 42

To day is a anaversery when lamb st got bomd. Two of the people were killed. Misis preisty was a maid, and also the little girls mother. Her farther was in work and only the little girl was saved. It was my father who fetched the Amblance. Our house was bomd. So we came over here (In my Grands) Well, that and a year ago, and a lot more too. Since then a lot have happend. My father have left us. Our landlord was to mingy [too mean] to do any thing. My father done our lavetry. And when my father told the landlord that he had done the job, she did not give him anything (He done a lot to this house without any thanks from our mingy landlord).

February 20th 1942
I have been to school today. I have had all my sum's right. I expect
I will be listening to Tommy Handly on the wireless tonight. It is
friday today it is twenty past five I am listenin-g to the children
hour.

February 21st 1942
I listend to Tommy Handly last night. I am listenen to Worker's
Canteen on the wireless. The time is 8 o'clock p.m. It is Satarday. I
did not go to town this morning to change my library book. Niether
have I seen my pal John Lewis. I expect I will listen to Music Hall
at quarter past 8 o'clock. I also went to the picture house, at first we
could not get in, so we went to Carlton picture house instead. It was
a good picture.

A four-year silence was to follow.

* * *

As it happened, I was not the only person in the house involved in
epistolary activities. My Father's departure from the Hafod did not
mean that he had dropped out of the picture altogether. He still
wrote me letters (as he preferred not to deal with my Mother
direct), but apart from that, my Mother wanted to keep in touch
with him for financial reasons. At first she had no job, and was very
dependent on the few shillings he sent over. It was not nearly
enough, so soon she started writing to ask for more. A new stage
had begun in their relationship.

The first of her letters was posted on the 3rd September 1941,
a few weeks after the separation; my Father stored them away
carefully, to be discovered only many years later when I went
through his papers. My Mother began her assault with a string of
recriminations.

Mr. W. A. Matthews
I am replying to the letter which you sent to Mervyn last weekend.
Please understand that I do not wish him to be depressed over
money matters. Several times since he had your letter he has told
me that he will keep himself out of his money-box money. So please
what you want me to know, do not write through the child.

Secondly, I took a temporary post as Comptometer Operator
over the holiday period for the simple reason that Mervyn and I
could not possibly exist on 25 shillings per week. It would be very
interesting if, this week-end you tried how you could get on on 25/-

to keep yourself in food, clubs, clothes, rent, coal, light. I have always had the name of starving you. The boot is on the other foot. It is Mervyn and I would have starved had I not gone to work, you starver. He wants a winter mack priced at 35s 11d at the Co-op. 10 shillings today is worth about as much as 5 shillings was 3 years ago.

If ever you feel like inquiring after me again, please do not refer to me as your "Misses" I always hated public house slang, as you know.

> Yours truly,
> L. Matthews.

The next two notes demanded money to pay for the storage of our furniture in our next-door neighbours' down (2s 6d a week), and contained the first of many threats.

Mervyn is getting a big boy [she wrote] and very sensitive and if you would send sufficient to keep him without going through Court, so much the better for him in later life. If I was only better off financially I would slash the 10 shillings in your false face.

P.S. you are also getting 'dole' for me of which I receive nothing. You had better be careful.

Mother said little to me about these letters, but in any case my Father had no intention of coughing up, and there was no noticeable change in the situation.

* * *

One small adventure remains to be recounted from my early days in the Hafod. Gran and my Mother rarely went out together, and Gran had ever greater difficulty in walking. But the three of us did have one little outing. One day, not long after we moved from Lamb Street, when Gran could still get around a bit, a letter came from Auntie Gerthie, who lived across the river Tawe in Pentrechwith. Her father, whom everyone called Uncle Dai, had been a Councillor before he died many years previously, but was well remembered in the family. Auntie Gerthie still kept the Post Office there.

"Oh," said Gran, "Gerthie have written and invited us to go and see them one evening. I haven't been over there for years. Is the boat still running?"

She meant the small open ferry which plied across the river near the Hafod. Generations of workmen (our family among them) had used the boat to cross to the old Hafodisha Works, when Swansea was still the copper centre of the world. The ferry saved long bus journeys down to the town girder bridge, and up the other side.

I had had no idea who Auntie Gerthie and her family were, but I had always dreamed of going on a boat. Since there was no hope of my ever having one, and I did not know anyone who did, my chances of getting afloat seemed non-existent. You could not sail in Swansea Bay, anyway – there was a war on. This was my chance.

"Oh Gran," I said. "I've never been on a boat! Let's all go!"

"I don't know whether I can manage it son, my legs are so bad."

But my eagerness carried the day, and we all decided to go. How exciting it was! Gran put on her very best outdoor clothes – a black silk coat and hat, the first time I had ever seen her in them. And on the appointed evening off we went, Gran leaning heavily on her stick and on my Mother's arm: down Maliphant Street, rough and unpaved, and under the smoky railway bridge at the bottom. Then over the shunting tracks, across the canal bridge with its cast-iron notice about Traction Engines, and down the long, narrow lane which led to the muddy, almost disused quay. The lane was bounded by high sandstone walls, Neath Road was distant, and there was nothing to be heard. It was eerie, as well as exciting. But we had to endure a dreadful stench which came (according to rumour) from the vats of a mysterious tripe factory. If that were so, it must have supplied the whole of Wales.

Some steps led down to a slippery wooden walk at the water's edge. The boatman sat in a little white house on the Pentrechwith side, waiting to be called out to sail the old boat over the thirty yards or so of water. Since there was a danger of it being swept away by the strong current (the river was still tidal there), the gunwale was attached by chain to a pulley which ran on a cable across the water.

I could not, that evening, have been less concerned about the history of the place, or family use in days gone by; this was to be my first boat trip ever. The boatman brought her over, and we clambered in. Gran could only just manage it, half-lifted by the boatman. I held on to the wet gunwale as we worked our way across the fast-moving, muddy flow. When we reached the other side we somehow got Gran out and made our way up the steep path to the main road. The slope of Kilvey Hill (where we now found ourselves) was moon-like in its desolation. Then there was the slow, slow walk to Pentrechwith itself, a forlorn, wind-swept little place with brown sandstone-and-clinker houses.

The Post Office was located in the parlour of one of them, and Auntie Gerthie's family lived in the kitchen at the back. They were glad to see us. The grown-ups spent the evening gossiping, while I played with a new-found cousin almost my own age. Strange snatches of conversation reached us.

"Bessy have gone flighty up in London," somebody said of Aunt Gerthie's daughter. "The police found her handbag after an air raid, and no one knows whether she's still alive."

"Well, if she's living on the street, like a prostitute," Auntie Gerthie declared, "I wouldn't care if she was dead!"

I was completely shocked.

The most astounding thing for me, however, was the weaponry. My cousin had not only an air pistol with a barrel which shot out when you pulled the trigger, but also, marvel of marvels, a real, working ten-chamber revolver. It was a gangster's gun, with a short, one-inch barrel made to fit snugly in the pocket. I wondered how on earth a thing like that had found its way into Pentrechwith.

It was pitch dark when we got back to the ferry: the only light came from a bare bulb hanging outside the boatman's cottage. The river had by now flooded, the water was fast-moving and inky. It covered the walk, and we had to step into the boat straight from the bank. This time there were other passengers, and the boat was down to its gunwales. Of course, we got over safely. As we made our way home I decided that visiting Pentrechwith was probably the most exciting thing I had ever done since I came to live in the Hafod.

Three

And So to School

When we moved to Gran's I had to go to the Hafod school. It was a large, pole-stone building on Odo Street, with railings and asphalt playing grounds. The boys' and girls' parts were quite separate. My Mother took me up one cold, miserable morning reminiscent of the time when I first went to Waun Wen. I had a good idea of what was coming, and a strong foreboding that (like Waun Wen school) it would be much less interesting than the world outside. We met the Headmaster, a straight-backed, white-haired old gent called Mr. Perry.

"Very glad to have the boy," he told my Mother, after listening to her tale. "We're lucky not to have had any bombing in the Hafod. We've already accepted several boys who've been bombed out in other parts of the town."

"The Headmaster in Waun Wen thought Mervyn would be a sure winner of the Scholarship," my Mother said proudly.

"Good, good," said Mr. Perry. "How old is he? He's got a year or two before that, hasn't he. Let's see how he gets on. He'll be starting in Mr. Richard's class." He offered my Mother a cup of tea and stirred it with a pencil, because the secretary had forgotten to bring a spoon. Afterwards my Mother kept telling people what a nice, homely person he was.

'Richie', as we called him, turned out to be an irascible little man who lived in a gaunt detached house but a few yards from the school itself. He gave cuffs across the ear which left you feeling giddy for hours. Once, after an especially painful blow, I got my Mother to write him a letter of complaint. It didn't help – he just complained to the other masters about getting it: I heard him talking about me.

His boys were already on pounds, shillings and pence, which were quite beyond me. Also, he made us write in pen and ink, and since I wasn't used to it, this made the work harder. Usually there wasn't enough ink powder for the class, so our writing came out like a brown tea stain. I felt thoroughly out of place and didn't pal up with any of the boys there. After a few weeks of wrong and fading answers Richie made me sit next to one of the best boys, so that I could learn from him.

Three problems were becoming apparent, though I had had a foretaste of them at Waun Wen. Later I thought of them as the three 'Bs'. The first was – *Boredom*! In the Hafod school lessons there was hardly anything of interest at all. To be fair, the staff were mostly over-aged, and struggling to cope with war duties, so they couldn't be expected to show much initiative. Richie made us learn unending stanzas of Wordsworth while he rested at his large oak desk in the corner; "I wandered lonely as a cloud" was recited again and again, in all its rhythmic horror, till going-home time. When the bell went I was always first out, a lone figure running down the street, fleeing from boredom. Why hang about in the playground when there were far more interesting things to do at home?

After a year with Richie, I passed up to 'Wiggy' Harris's class. Wiggy was a frail, dark man with a few thin locks of greying hair combed carefully over his scalp. The fact that they never moved led us to believe that they were pasted on, hence the nickname. Here I ran up against my second 'B' problem. P.T. (Physical Training) – lessons were held in the assembly hall, for we had no gymnasium. When our first class came along Wiggy ordered us to kneel on the parquet floor and tumble over. I found, to my horror that I simply couldn't tumble. I was perfectly healthy, but my body wouldn't do it! I sat on the floor, guilt-ridden, looking at my classmates' legs flailing as they went over and over again. Wiggy came up to me, curious.

"Can't you tumble?" he asked, loud and in front of the whole class. "Why ever not?"

There was a great burst of laughter. Perhaps Wiggy believed that a little ridicule would help, but it only made things worse. Later in the same class I had to draw a chalk line between two rows of boys, walking backwards. I just couldn't get it straight.

"Are you drawing a straight line, or an elephant?" the teacher asked. There was another gust of merriment. The dreadful truth was now becoming apparent to me (and everyone else): I was *Bad at PT*, and probably at games as well. And there was no brother or father at hand to teach me. I had never played football at Waun Wen, and began in the Hafod by kicking the ball into the nearest goal, which happened to be our own. Subsequently, I was always the last to be called when a team was being made up. During playtime I would mostly run around the yard alone, pretending to be a 0-6-0 tank engine or a tram. I remember, one bright sunny morning, looking at my shadow on the asphalt, and thinking: Why am I alone?

Nothing much of interest happened in Wiggy's class, either. A classmate inadvertently knocked the corner off my front tooth while I was swigging from a milk-bottle during the eleven o'clock break. A trainee teacher came and tried to get us to do a sketch from *Oliver Twist* while Mr. Harris looked on, warming himself against the radiator. I was supposed to be the Artful Dodger, but the teacher left before we could put it on. Meanwhile Mr. Lewis, the ubiquitous Welsh teacher, came once a week and tried to teach us bits of that strange language. He would stand in front of us, put his hands on his head, and say, in all seriousness, "Dyma fy nhwylo ar fy mhen". The whole class ached with boredom or concealed mirth. We all came from English-speaking families, anyway.

By this time, however, the third problem was making itself felt, namely, *bullying*. At Waun Wen I had once controlled it by challenging my tormentor to a fight, and beating him. The boys in the Hafod, however, were a much tougher lot, and for some reason scared me. I soon found myself at the end of the line for threats and punches, with nobody I could bully in turn. The other boys sensed my timidity, and (I sometimes felt) were surprised by it. After being hit in the playground by a swarthy boy called Lewis Saunders for some unintended slight, a challenge to 'put up your mits' made my stomach turn over.

I was not fitting in at Hafod school. So what had gone wrong? Perhaps even one successful pugilistic encounter – for example, giving someone a black eye – would have turned the scales for ever, but it was not to be. Sometimes I would think about it. In Lamb Street my Mother had always encouraged me to keep to myself: perhaps that's what started it. Maybe the fearsome air raids, the bombing of our home, the move to the Hafod, and my Father's absence had an unnerving effect on me. The John Bevan episode in Lamb Street did not help, either. Sometimes people commiserated with me for being an only child; "You get soft and spoilt, see." Though tall, I was (as my Mother told me repeatedly) rather delicate and incapable of rough behaviour.

My interests, moreover, seemed to lie not in games and gang activities, like most other boys', but in practical, creative things, or in reading. That is where, increasingly, I found my pleasures. I also liked old things. Lewis Saunders, for instance, one day amazed me by coming to school with a beautiful nineteenth-century pocket pistol which he had got heaven knows where. But he had no idea of how to look after it, and a few days later I saw it lying broken on his desk. Why hadn't he taken care of it? No one seemed concerned about it – except me.

* * *

The last, and most important class in the school was 'Bouncer' Hughes's, important because it contained the boys who were doing the scholarship exam so as to get into a grammar school. Later it was called the 'Eleven Plus'. My Mother was desperate for me pass up, so into Mr. Hughes's scholarship group I went. In the school vestibule, high up on the wall, was the Board of Honour on which the successful candidates' names had been painted in letters of gold, and my Mother spoke of it in an awed voice. By the time I got to that level the practice had been abandoned, perhaps because no gold paint was available in wartime.

'Bouncer' was the word we used for 'boaster', and Hughsie (his other nick-name) did little else. He was a tense, flabby man with an unsightly mole on his cheek who usually came to school in pin-striped suits which seemed to emphasise his fatness. One of his favourite pastimes was telling us how much people valued his service in the Fire Brigade, where he was a part-time officer.

He was also something of a disciplinarian and gave us 'cracks' on the hand with a bamboo cane. The instrument was split, and particularly painful for that reason. You were most likely to get a crack around mid-morning, during arithmetic lessons, when the well-thumbed answer-book was circulating, and things could get a bit out of hand. You were supposed to do your sums, check your own answer, then go to his desk to show him your workings.

"Mervyn Matthews," he said one day, peering at my brown ink figures, "the working is wrong, you couldn't possibly have got the right answer that way. You must have looked it up. And you're one of the Scholarship boys, too."

"Well, Sir..."

"Did you look at the answer book before you did the sum!"

I had seen the answer by chance, but I nodded negatively.

"Put your hand out!" he said, reaching for his cane. The usual crack followed, and I returned to my desk clutching a painful palm.

The desks of the classroom were arranged in blocks, and Hughsie seated his boys roughly according to ability. So you moved up or down according to your marks. The bottom block contained the dunces and ne'er-do-wells, including a boy who had been caught stealing on Neath Road and always smelt of gravy. A poor half-wit called Gordon sat there also, because there was nowhere else for him to go. He troubled no one, unless teased beyond measure, or chased, when he could get violent.

The top block, nearest the window, was occupied by the Scholarship boys. As the months went by, the top block worked away in dread anticipation of the exam. Sometimes, but not very often, Hughsie would give us bits of homework. We thought that perhaps his fire duties limited the time he had for marking. Mr. Perry, who had become ever more ghost-like, was replaced by a Mr. Morgan, stout, jolly and alert. He showed a keen interest in the Scholarship group, and our work seemed to pick up a little. When the day came we took the exam in Swansea Grammar School. Afterwards the inevitable disaster stories circulated amongst the mothers. Glenys Lloyd, who lived down the street, had come home distraught. "Our Glenys was crying like a bull," her Mother told me, "she thinks she did very badly." I was surprised because I had never heard of a bull crying. My cousin Betty who lived in Treboeth had turned over two pages of questions without noticing, and had apparently finished her paper far too early to pass. As for me, I wasn't at all sure how I had done.

Then one morning, some weeks before the result was due, a letter arrived from the Guildhall. What could it be? My Mother opened it quickly. The news was mixed: I had not passed the exam, but I had not failed, either. I was a borderline case, and was being called for a further interview at the Grammar School. I went down at the appointed time, and two teachers questioned me about my answers. I came away with no idea of how things had gone.

The dénouement came before we broke up. One morning Mr. Morgan came into the classroom and smilingly interrupted the lesson. "Can I have a word with them, Mr. Hughes? ...Yes, boys, the scholarship results are in." We all held our breath and stared at him.

"I think we should all congratulate Tony Wallace," he said. "He has passed his Scholarship and got a place at Swansea Grammar School."

Hughsie sat silently at his desk, he may have known already. The boys in the top block exchanged glances. Tony Wallace? Tony Wallace? Why only him? One boy out of ten! What about the other best boys? Billy Lewis, John Waters, me... The disappointment was scarcely bearable.

But it would have been quite wrong for any of us to look disappointed, so we put a brave face on it and congratulated Tony. Then: "Hughsie's been giving Tony private lessons," someone whispered. In a flash it all became clear. Once, in class, Hughsie had quietly asked Tony Wallace about some homework, and those of us who overheard the remark were puzzled because he hadn't given us any.

So Tony's parents must have paid for extra tuition – nobody else could afford it. Tony's unique feat became understandable: and the person who came off worst was Hughsie. He had nine failures to answer for.

After breaking the news, Mr. Morgan called me aside.

"Mervyn," he said, "Your mother has just been up to the school specially to get the results. She was disappointed, but she took it very well. How lucky you are to have a Mother like that...."

Need I add that all hell was waiting for me when I got home for dinner.

"You silly fool," my Mother shouted. "You're always towards the top of the class, aren't you? One of the best boys? What went wrong, then? Here am I working my fingers to the bone... Thumping that old comptometer all day... I often thought that old Hughesie wasn't giving you enough homework! Dishonest bugger! And all the hours you spends in the shed don't help, either. Oh, my Gawd. You failed."

The thought that I had done my best, and things were pretty difficult at home, anyway, never entered her head. Gran went on cooking in the back kitchen, unperturbed.

"I can try again when I'm twelve," I retorted.

"If you didn't make it at eleven, you won't stand a chance at twelve. They make it harder the second time round."

The row ended with me feeling more miserable than ever. One thing, though – I knew there would be no trouble from my Father when I next saw him. He hardly knew what the Scholarship was. And indeed, when I next went over to St. Thomas and told him, he just tried to sound superior.

"I know what it's all about, Son," he said, with a knowing grin. "I've done it all."

"Done it all?" my Mother said, when I passed his comment on. "Done it all? The bloody liar. The only exam he ever took was to be a telegraph boy in the Post Office!"

However... all was not quite lost. In the days that followed a strange calm settled over No. 64, and even the squabbling with Gran subsided. My Mother was apparently occupied with other things. Rather to my surprise, she did not keep on and on about my failure, but started making unexplained visits to the Guildhall. Tales about our late Uncle Dai, the councillor from Pentrechwith, had taught her that much was to be gained from going to the focus of power. Then one day she returned triumphant.

"I've got some good news," she proclaimed. "They told me in

the Guildhall that as a borderline boy you have the chance of a place in Gwendraeth Valley School, near Crosshands. But it's only for Swansea evacuees, so you'll have to be evacuated down there. I suppose they've got room because people don't like their children leaving home. But it's better than nothing, isn' it?"

So that was that: I was going to be an evacuee, and pass up to a grammar school after all. I wondered what awaited me next.

★ ★ ★

My Gwendraeth adventure started one sunny morning in September, 1944. The thirty or so boys and girls (it was to be a mixed class) had been asked to assemble outside the Guildhall. My Mother and I arrived to find a group of parents and children standing expectantly around the single-decker bus which had been hired to take us to our various 'billets'. The only person I knew, quite by chance, was a skinny little boy called John Halfpenny, who was also there with his Mother. Despite the bright sunshine and the excitement, some of the Mothers were nearly weeping. When we climbed into the bus and the driver started the engine, my own could stand it no longer, and burst into tears. Consoling gestures through the window, and the sure knowledge that I would be back in the Hafod around 5 o'clock on Friday, were of no avail. Gwendraeth was only 18 miles away, but the distance seemed enormous.

My Mother had taken the precaution of asking the master in charge, Mr. Glan Powell, to place me with a good family, and he had specially recommended a Mr. and Mrs Anthony. The Anthonys were, he said, a middle-aged couple living with their grown-up daughter Mary, who had trained to be a teacher. An hour or so after leaving Swansea I was duly deposited in their detached house on the main road outside Crosshands. It had a little grocer's shop in the front room and an enormous garden behind.

I was warmly greeted. Mrs. Anthony was a white-haired, kind-hearted woman, whose surplus fat shook visibly when she moved. She was a former nurse, who (I learned later) had tragically lost a son just as he was about to graduate as a Baptist minister. "I thought that having an evacuee in the house would help her get over it," Mary told me, "take her mind off things." Mary was an attractive, charming girl who would have made a wonderful sister. She practised Mozart on the piano and had a Morris 8 car (although it was only the model with the built-in headlamps, which I disliked).

Her Father was a red-faced collier, also white-haired and slightly irascible; he drove the winding-engine at Blaenhirwaun Colliery, half a mile away, tended the garden, and looked after their pig. He also kept the latrine in order, strewing its malodrous contents over the vegetable plots. His first name was Ivan, pronounced Eevan, which I had never heard before, and after I had been there a few days he tried to teach me Welsh, starting with 'Yes' and 'No'. But since the grammar was difficult, and he didn't know it anyway, we didn't get very far. Everybody normally spoke Welsh, and small children knew no English.

Although their house was relatively new, the Anthony's kitchen had a large black range with an open fire which Mrs. Anthony used for cooking, much as we did in the Hafod. The little shop sold cigarettes to the colliers and food to their families, so the front of the house was often quite busy. The Anthonys did all they could to make me feel at home, but their way of life was quite different from what I had been used to. There were no close neighbours, no family rows, and everybody seemed to get on famously. The food was skimpy and mostly slap-dash, with none of the carefully cooked things I enjoyed in the Hafod.

There was also a big problem with the sleeping arrangements. Mrs. Anthony put cotton sheets on the beds, such as we never used in the Hafod, and I was always freezing at night. I was ashamed to tell Mrs. Anthony that we slept in blankets. Apart from that the bed stood right in front of a window with thin curtains, and the morning light always woke me early. The discomfort provoked a recurring dream that my genitals had turned into a frog. When I opened my eyes, I saw, instead of the pole-stone houses opposite, a long garden, with dismal, misty fields beyond: for Gwendraeth seemed to be even more rain-washed than Swansea.

The day was ordered quite differently, too. It would start with Mrs. Anthony calling out to me in Welsh, "Tyrd yma, fy machgen i", I would get out of bed, dress on the cold bedroom mat and wash in the bathroom. Downstairs Mrs. Anthony would give me a good breakfast, usually salt bacon and a few chips from a pan balanced precariously on the coals. This was definitely the best meal of the day. I would eat it at the kitchen table, while Mary played her Mozart in the next room. Then I would collect my books and go out to the bus stop to wait for the old single-decker that delivered me to the school, a mile or so away.

The problem was getting on the damn thing. I was not particularly agile, and the driver would never actually stop just for one passenger, perhaps to save the wear on the brakes. He would slow to what he thought matched a fast run, and I was expected to leap on to the step as the bus coasted past. I hated it.

At school, the Swansea evacuees had their own classroom at the end of a long corridor. The local boys spoke Welsh and regarded us as outsiders, so all in all we were not much involved in mainstream school life. School work at Gwendraeth, I found, was hardly less boring than at the Hafod, despite the new subjects. We had Shakespeare (who wrote peculiar English) with 'Fanny' Williams, physics (mostly incomprehensible) with Bingo Price, and mathematics with a thin irascible master whose name I forget. He once went berserk on account of the noise in the class, and dashed around hitting everyone on the head with his disintegrating textbook. After he calmed down we helped him to pick up the pages. But there were bright moments, too. The school choir met close by and did a wonderful renderings of Welsh folk songs, including 'Dafydd y Garreg Wen': it was the first time I ever heard this overpoweringly beautiful melody.

There was less bullying, but sport continued to be a major bugbear. My heart sank when I saw the gym master, who was young, strong and obviously enthusiastic. His main form of torture was making us run from one side of the gym to the other and clamber to the top of the wall bars. The slowest boy had his name called out after each burst, and it was usually me. Then there was the tall boy with one leg, who somehow managed to play cricket better than I could with two.

The morning's work might present no great difficulty, but lunchtime was dreadful. Mrs. Anthony naturally thought that I would be satisfied with school dinners, having no idea of how pampered I was at home. The disgusting taste of the Gwendraeth mashed potato and paraffin-scented gravy was to remain with me for life: God knows what went into it! The upshot, after a few weeks of suffering, was a letter from my Mother to the Anthony household, asking if I could have sandwiches instead. Mrs. Anthony, kind but uncomprehending, began to give me unappetising wedges of bread and jam, so as often as not I went hungry. The evening meal at my new home was nothing to look forward to, either; I found to my astonishment that Mr. Anthony was perfectly happy with a plate of boiled swede and green peas, though I usually did a little better.

The only good food I had at Gwendraeth was the lunches I brought down from Swansea on a Monday morning – pasties which had been cooked the day before, or lovely fresh meat sandwiches with mustard. Sometimes, if it was not actually raining, I would take them down to the local LMS railway siding, clamber into one of the unattended railway carriages, and eat them in the comparative luxury of a third-class compartment. Of course, you always had to be on the look-out for railway staff, and if there was an engine nearby there was a danger of being shunted off... Fortunately, it never quite happened.

Inevitably, the best part of the week was leaving for home on a Friday afternoon. If we were well-behaved we might be allowed to take the slightly earlier, and faster bus which went through Tumble village. As time went by, it became our habit to get our coats on before school finished, and before long we were spending the last three lessons fully dressed and ready to go. One day Glan Powell came in and saw us. His gold spectacles glinted with indignation. "Why is everybody dressed to go home?" he thundered. "You've got another two classes yet. Get those coats off straight away!" No early bus that day.

* * *

The evenings at Gwendraeth, unlike the days, were full of fascination. Crosshands was surrounded by coal mines with steam engines, and usually, as soon as I had finished my homework, I would set off to explore them. Not for me escapades in the empty fields or moisture-laden woods, like the other boys: I sought rather the puff of steam rising above the engine-house, the smell of warm oil, the excitement of spinning metal.

I began with Blaenhirwaun Colliery, which was the nearest. The main winding-engine, which Mr. Anthony drove, was a black witch of a thing turning an incredibly large and greasy cable drum. The cables passed through an aperture in the corrugated iron roof, and disappeared into the sky beyond, eventually reaching the great wheels above the pit shaft. The engineman had to stand on a wooden platform and divide his attention between the steam throttle, a gigantic footbrake, and the reverse lever. A bell signal told him when to start, and a weighted cord, wound over the main axle, showed the position of the cages in the shaft. It was all very simple, and left a lot to the engineman's judgement. After I had seen Mr. Anthony do it a few times, I plucked up courage and asked if I could have a go.

"Duw annwyl," he said angrily, "No, you can't." He tut-tutted at the thought.

A little setback like that did not, however, dim my enthusiasm. I still had the boiler-house, the various small donkey engines, the lamp room, and the pithead with its iron gates. No one seemed to object to a twelve-year old boy hanging around. It was not long before I discovered the shed where the four-wheeled shunting engine was kept, hiding behind its own over-sized buffers. At that hour there was no one to stop me climbing into the cabin, and handling all the levers. Usually it still had steam up, some fifty pounds or so: to make it go, you only needed to unscrew the hand-brake, lean on the throttle, and...

Fortunately, I never dared. In terms of engine driving I did, however, enjoy an exhilarating five minutes at "The Slant" mine in Tumble. One evening I got there to find their 0-4-0 standing at the head of a line of trucks, loaded and ready to depart. I scrambled over the uneven lines to the edge of the footplate, and looked up into the cab. The driver, a young man, smiled at me.

"Can I have a go at driving?" I said.

"Yes," he answered to my delight. "Climb in."

I climbed up the iron footholds and entered the small mechanical heaven, with its levers, gauges, hissing steam, odd drips, and a furnace roaring underneath the boiler. There was a tiny bunker for coal. I tugged open the throttle (it was very stiff) and the engine started with a jolt. We began to pull up the incline. A moment later, to my great consternation, the engine lurched and stopped moving: the wheels span uselessly without purchase. They had slipped off the rails and settled in the dirt. I closed the throttle and looked at the driver in alarm: but he wasn't in the least perturbed.

"It's always happening," he grinned again. "It's these old rails, see."

He jumped down and I followed him to watch. Grabbing two pieces of iron from the footplate he thrust them under the displaced front wheels. We got back into the cab, and after a few moments of grinding and shuddering in reverse the 0-4-0 was back on the lines. I took over the throttle again and we continued our laborious way up the incline. Not many boys could have actually driven a steam engine I thought, and wondered what John Lewis would say when I told him.

As for the winding engines, the pistons, sliding rods, eccentrics, and valves presented an unending variety. The engine-men at different collieries soon got to know me, and welcomed my appearances. "Hello, boy, come around again have you? Brought your sister for me this time, have you?" My favourite engine was much more delicately built than the others; it had, I was told, given many years' service on a paddle steamer in the Bristol Channel. The eccentrics on the main shaft were spoked, rather than solid, and the cranks and driving rods thinner, so as to save weight.

The oldest of the winding engines had drop-valves, which were raised by steam-driven levers, and fell back with a thump under the force of gravity. The trouble with them, it seemed, was that they could jam if they got dirty, and stop the engine dead – which could be nasty for anybody who happened to be in the cages. Some old bricks were tied to the top of them to avoid that contingency. The only engine I really disliked was the electrical thing which worked the slag-tip trolley at Blaenhirwaun. It had masses of cogs, and made a terrible noise. The man who worked it, however, had artistic leanings, and one of the walls of the engine house was decorated with a large three-quarter length drawing of a girl standing naked before an oval mirror. You did not fail to notice the fuzz along the lower edge of the frame.

★ ★ ★

Yes, sex was coming into the picture, and provoking furtive, but ever more compelling discussion at school. Most boys took it for granted that when the time came, your father would take you into the parlour and explain 'It' without dirty words. (I could not possibly imagine my Father doing anything of the sort.) But there was much to be learnt from friends as well.

"Your Mother and Father have been doing It for years, you nut. Otherwise you wouldn't be here, would you?" A sallow boy called Hewitt, who was a bit older than the rest of us, demonstrated the motion with a loose drain pipe stanchion which fitted a hole in the school wall. "Just like that."

A number of potent new words found their way into our vocabulary while some common ones acquired new meanings. If someone said, for instance, "They've got you by the short and curlies?" you knew exactly what it meant. The Bible also had dirty bits, like 'spilling your seed' and 'Sodom and Gomorrah', and one or two boys knew where to look them up. Another place was the Doctor's Book in the parlour, if you had one: need I add that some of the pages in the Aberdyberthi Street copy got well-thumbed.

There was a great deal of puzzlement about how long It took, estimates ranging from a minute or so to an hour and a half. Skin colour raised questions as well, for there were no Chinese or Negro boys around to tell you. Somebody said that Chinese came off yellow, and Negroes – black, which is why their children were the same colour. The sinfulness of It all was unquestioned, and attested by every chapel in Wales. The girls at Gwendraeth had their own conclaves, and one was heard to say that she was "never going to have any, now she knew how they done it".

★ ★ ★

At nine o'clock on the evening of Monday, 7th May, the great news came over the wireless: Victory had been declared in Europe, and the war was (in effect) over. There was only one thought in my mind: get back to Swansea to see what was going on! All the evacuees at Gwendraeth would be doing the same thing. There were to be two days of national celebration and the school would probably be closed, anyway.

After a breathless word to Mrs. Anthony I ran the mile to the bus-stop in Crosshands, in the hope of catching the last bus home. It had gone, so I left for Swansea first thing next morning. The weather was fair, and I arrived in Aberdyberthi Street to find preparations for a street 'do' well advanced. Some trestle tables covered with white cloths had been set up and later that afternoon there would be tea, cakes, jelly and blancmange.

As the hour approached, the excitement grew. There were a few benches, but some people had to take their own chairs. A surprising variety of seating appeared, from stools to the best mahogany. Word went around that pensioners and people who could not walk would have their tea taken in to them. I rushed in to tell Gran.

"Don't worry, Gran," I said. "You won't miss anything. They'll be bringing tea around for the old people."

"Oh, there's nice," she replied, and her face lit up. "Go and get one of them clean tea-clothes from the kitchen, and I'll have it on my knees."

I brought the cloth, and she spread it out in preparation. She got very little in the way of treats, and was really looking forward to it. My Mother, withdrawn as always, didn't take much interest, so I went down the street alone, lugging my chair. By then the tables were almost fully occupied, the spaces at the ends, from where the food would be served, having been taken up first.

We were supposed to start with the jelly, but before long the worried looks of the women dishing it out showed that there was not enough to go around. In fact, there wasn't enough of anything, and the people in the middle of the table ended up looking at one another over empty plates. I carried my chair back to No. 64.

"I'm sorry Gran," I said, "there wasn't enough to go around."

She started to cry softly, as she so often did.

"I've lived here so many years," she said, "and I was looking forward to it. I've been simpled."

I'd never heard the expression before.

"Don't worry," I said, as I smoothed her forehead. "It's only a bit of jelly and cake. We've got plenty of food in the house, haven't we?"

Some street entertainments had been organised to follow. There was a motorbike-decorating competition, which was won by a young lady who packed the spokes of her enormously powerful machine with sprigs of lilac. The agreeable impression which the show of blossom created was, however, banished from my head just before the slow cycle race, when my cousin Gordon gave me a wallop because I pointed out that he had the unfair advantage of a low gear mechanism. He was stronger and more aggressive than I, so once again retaliation was impossible. The children's fancy-dress competition was judged by the vicar from the Church of England up in Odo Street, where hardly anyone went. He gave a prize to a bewildered two-year-old dressed up as a pixy. Later, there was a dance and fancy dress in the mission hall, and Auntie Enid did the hokey-kokey with Mr. Gardener. My Mother donned my Uncle Jack's suit and a trilby. "Ma, you look ridiculous!" I said as she gazed at herself in the mirror. But she went nevertheless.

★ ★ ★

When we all got back to Gwendraeth we were told that the evacuation arrangement would be terminated, and next term we would all be transferred to schools in Swansea. By this time, however, life had begun to unravel a bit at the billet. Mrs. Anthony had stopped asking me to serve in the shop, because I didn't always wash my hands, and as a former State-Registered Nurse, she disliked the black marks I left on the lard. When I inadvertently broke the crucifix on one of Mary's necklaces, and forgot to apologise, she was justifiably annoyed. My circumstances at home in the Hafod also cast a shadow and (I suspect) made the Anthonys a bit suspicious of me.

"Dear Billie," my Mother wrote in one of her letters to my Father, "I was very upset to learn that the Anthonys in Crosshands have found out we are separated, and that Mervyn is from a broken home. There was no need for that. Perhaps he said something to them."

Finally I got myself involved in some sort of scrape with one of the local boys; Mrs. Anthony's letter box had its spring broken; and one of the neighbours complained that I was a Bad Influence. That was too much for Mr. Anthony.

"You can bloody well go home," he told me through a mouthful of peas (or was it swede?), after the complaint came in.

"Oh Ivan," said Mrs. Anthony, kind as ever, "don't speak to the boy like that!"

"Well, he can."

My record was not too bad for an evacuated twelve year-old, but Mrs. Anthony did have a word with me when we were alone.

"I think, bachgen i," she said, "the trouble with you is, you're not fit!"

"Fit, Mrs. Anthony?"

There was nothing I could say because I did not understand her. I knew I was perfectly healthy, even if bad at games. Perhaps she was using a Welsh turn of phrase? However, time maketh all things clear, and I later came to believe that she meant something like 'assertive', or 'resilient', perhaps like her son. Yet despite the circumstances of my departure we remained on good terms, and in later years my Mother would send me down to the Anthonys to buy the Christmas chicken. And they always made me welcome. In one respect, however, possibly the most important, my year at Gwendraeth ended very well. When the exam results were out I found I had come third in the class, justifying my Mother's high expectations.

"So the boy's coming back home," said Gran, obviously pleased. "Ugh, all that bloody education! I don' hold with it!"

* * *

When the summer holiday came to its unwanted end I started at my fourth school, Dynevor Secondary Modern. Dynevor had been my first choice for a Scholarship place, as my Uncle Jack had gone there, and I was anxious to follow in his footsteps. The school colours – red and yellow stripes on black – had a friendly glow about them. It was located right in the centre of town, at the bottom of Mount Pleasant Hill, only twenty minutes' walk from the Hafod. The premises adjoined the Albert Hall cinema on one side, and Mount Pleasant Chapel, the local fount of Baptist fervour, on the other. The buildings had suffered badly during the blitzes, and the middle part, together with most of an upper story, had been destroyed. Many of the classrooms had damp ceilings, stained plaster, and make-shift windows.

When one writes of one's boyhood one naturally tries to pick out the most interesting bits, skipping over the welter of boredom and the dross. So I shall not have much to say about my first year at Dynevor. They put me in form 3C, in one of the less damaged areas, but I soon realised that I was again in for a boring time. The best master we had was the deputy head, Mr. Davies, who taught history. However, he had a weakness for headings, sub-headings, and telegram-style notes, and left most of the interesting detail for perusal in later life. Things got worse when, as a result of a timetable change, he was replaced by another, smaller Mr. Davies who had been with us at Gwendraeth. He was a lazy man, and I shall never forget seeing him at his desk making plastic bangles while a boy read aloud from one of the textbooks.

Another Mr. Davies, a turkey-necked little man, quickly demonstrated that English could be extraordinarily uninteresting as well.

"Now boys," he would say in his strong Swansea drawl, "today it's going to be parzin'." 'Parzin' was the grammatical analysis of sentences, and we would spend the next hour in a tedious contemplation of subordinate clauses.

Art was taught by a quiet individual called Sandy Morgan. He was chiefly known for his method of preserving discipline, which involved walking around the class with a short, heavy stick and dropping one end of it on the heads of the most troublesome offenders. It hurt dreadfully. Mathematics was taught by a short, dark-haired man in glasses which vastly enlarged his eyes, and earned him the title of Tojo, after (I believe) a Japanese general. The intricacies of German grammar were propounded by Mr. Yates, or Yato. He was hard-working teacher, but had great difficulty in enthusing us, not least because our outdated grammar book was set in dense Gothic lettering which we could hardly read. And I could never quite understand why, being so involved with the German language, he had not been arrested when war broke out, like Greco. Gymnastics were the usual nightmare, because I could not jump over the horse: fortunately, Dynevor had no playing fields of its own, so that sports were organised only one afternoon a term, up Townhill. If you kept your head down, you didn't get caught up in anything.

There were only two classes I really enjoyed. One was music, or more precisely, learning choral parts for the annual school concert in the Brangwyn Hall. This event was born of the enthusiasm of the music master, Mr. Gwilym Roberts, who liked conducting large choirs in front of large audiences, while his buxom wife, clad in a loud floral dress, played the piano. To this end, silly things like musical appreciation, theory and instrument-learning were banished from the syllabus. I spent my entire first year at Dynevor learning pieces of Handel, Haydn and Verdi, lead by Mr. Roberts' squeaky fiddle. The other class I came to like, for unknown reasons, was 'Scruff' Griffith's French. My new friend, Brinley Clifford (or 'Milky' as we called him), a neat diminutive boy, liked it as well, and when the morning break came, we would walk around the yard together, trying to converse in it, instead of playing games. If I heard anyone speak French in the street (sailors off the docks, for example) I would get very excited and approach them. I took a few French stories home and translated them aloud for Gran as she sat by the fire. She showed a most flattering interest.

A few other impressions. "The inspectors are coming next week, and we must show the school at its best," Mr. W. Bryn Thomas, the Headmaster, declared one morning from the pulpit of Mount Pleasant, where we gathered for assembly. (There was a little entrance to the chapel from the school yard.) "We must put our best foot forward." In the event everything possible was done to give a rosy and totally false impression of our activities. Mr. Davies the bangle-maker actually gave us a history essay to write, and Mr. Roberts spent a whole hour teaching us musical notation. But when the inspectors left everything reverted to normal, with (for me) the usual three 'B's'.

Indeed, bullying was back with a vengeance, somehow I seemed to attract it. One day I found myself in the yard being pushed from side to side of a ring of jeering boys. I didn't know who organised the ring, someone I offended inadvertently, I suppose: but I had never seen anyone jostled like that before, and I was quite upset. There was also a little fun, though, particularly the surreptitious fly-ripping which went on in the basement cloak room. One boy would rush up to another and catch him unawares, rip his flies open, and then disappear with a shriek of "Your hobby's showing" behind the coats. Everybody enjoyed it, but sometimes Bryn Thomas would go snooping there to try and catch the culprits.

* * *

The most interesting part of the school day, was, as always, going home at four o'clock. I had two regular ports of call. The first was Swansea Public Library, which I joined soon after we moved to the Hafod. It shared a large brick building with the Art School, the Fire Brigade and the Police Station. Whenever I went there I would look in reverently at the Reference Room, with its mahogany alcoves, glass bookcases, and spiral metal stairway. The Junior Section was shabby but functional, with a woman at the issue desk ever fingering through long boxes of membership cards.

I decided fairly early that I would concentrate on the 'William' stories by Richmal Crompton. John Lewis had read some, and told me they were good. My own impression was immediately favourable. So for the first few months of my membership I haunted the 'C' shelf, and eventually worked my way through the entire series. I liked William because though middle class, he was unassuming and not at all sporty. After a time I tried to compose my own William story. The plot now escapes me, but I managed to persuade John to write it out while I dictated. He had a fine sloping hand, and did it beautifully. A pity it all got smudged in an argument about whether the ink was dry.

When the 'Williams' were finished, I switched to pirate stories, starting with a couple of readings of *Treasure Island*. The absence of books at home, and the difficulty of getting books I liked, meant that I usually read each volume at least twice. For some years my world of fiction was peopled almost entirely by eighteenth-century seafarers, one-legged, one-eyed or partially palsied, and sensible young cabin-boys. There were ornately-sterned galleons, flint-lock muskets, and treasure chests. How humdrum life in the Hafod seemed by comparison.

The stock of pirate stories having been exhausted, I passed on to slightly more modern watery tales; windjammers with four mates and clean-limbed midshipmen. An impressive amount of detail about rigging and spars lodged in my mind. A great-grandfather of mine had apparently been a bargee, and my grandfather, Gamma's husband, had actually worked on sailing ships when they docked. Yet the closest I ever got to seafaring myself at that time (apart from my memorable crossing of the Tawe) were bike rides around Swansea docks.

Other kinds of boys' stories, including the antics of Biggles, the aircraft pilot, attracted me not at all, and I positively hated yarns about rich public schoolboys and cricket elevens. When it seemed that I had read all the maritime tales in the town, a sea-change came over my habits and I started the long, pleasurable haul through

Dickens. *Pickwick Papers* was my first choice; I began to read it while I was eating at the kitchen table, which for some reason annoyed my Mother greatly.

"For Gawd's sake stop reading at the table, will you?" she would say, as if the table were anything but the mess it was, what with the milk bottle, stains and crumbs. "That book will knock something over."

I rigged up an extra, and probably dangerous, light for reading in bed.

My second port of call on my way home was Ralph's Second-hand Bookshop. Much of the area around High Street Station had been destroyed by the bombing, but Ralph was fortunate in occupying one of the few undamaged sites. The front of his shop was taken up by a newspaper counter at which, day after day, sat a strikingly handsome woman. I marvelled at her abundant black chevelure, and the artistry which had clearly been lavished on her visage. Somebody once told me that she was Ralph's wife, but she looked more like a showbiz personality to me. Ralph himself was a tall, shabbily-dressed chap with an unexpectedly welcoming smile. He was usually to be found fussing about inside. He came to know me well.

"Any new sea stories in, Ralph?" I would ask, as I went in. "Or anything in French?"

"'Ave a look by the door," he might respond. "I think some stuff came in yesterday."

The books which were of most interest to me ranged in price from about nine pence to two and six, so I could manage to buy perhaps one a week. Inside, shelves of volumes on all subjects reached from floor to ceiling, with an extra block in the middle. Although Ralph knew no Welsh, he had a tendency to acquire expansive Welsh sermons which took up a lot of space. A rather irritable girl kept the stock under a hawkish gaze, and checked the prices when the browsers bought something. "You've paid for that, have you?" she might snap.

I never dared tell my Father that I went to Ralph's Bookshop, for although he never read anything, and would pinch any old stuff from the dock, his fastidiousness precluded the purchase of second-hand books. This did not mean, of course, that he would give me money for new ones. When he once sent me ten shillings for my birthday I spent it on a few of Ralph's volumes, and inscribed them 'From Dad, with Love', without telling him.

★ ★ ★

Nothing in my life was nearly as interesting as the events related in the books I read. But at the beginning of 1946 I again felt an urge to start a diary, perhaps in the hope that I might have an adventure or two worth recording. (In fact I did, a little later, though not at all what I wanted.) This time round I was more purposeful, and kept the entries going for nearly a year and a half.

Friday January 11th 1946
I, Mervyn Matthews, being thirteen years and five months of age, do hereby start the pages of this diary.
   I did not go out this afternoon but stayed in for the coal [delivery]. For the fifth time it did not come. Most of the afternoon I spent looking up the family history. I got as far back as 1802. We are having very bad weather.

[The 'family history' consisted of a few births and deaths entered on the fly-leaf of a dusty copy of *Hanes yr Eglwys Gristionogol Drwy y Byd.*]
   On the whole, my boyish pen, limited and repetitious, makes poor reading: but some of the pages I wrote retain a certain freshness. I recorded bicycle trips into the countryside, taking Gran's rations up to Treboeth (she stayed at Auntie Annie's from time to time), walking up to Mayhill with John Lewis, managing the chickens in the garden (they fought interminably) buying spare parts for my bike, trying to get my fountain pen to work, tests at school, choir practice in the Brangwyn Hall, and doing jigsaw puzzles (which I loved). There were accounts of fragile carpentry, paint which never dried, and cutting my wrist badly in the garden, (a stitch at the doctor's, to my Mother's horror, cost 7s 6d – about 37 pence in today's money). Some of my Mother's activities – a pious visit to Mount Pleasant Chapel, her part-time job doing census work, a Labour Party meeting – were all duly noted: how she and Auntie Annie distempered the kitchen yellow, and how we had a food parcel (under some sort of war assistance scheme) from unknown friends in Durban.
   Occasionally there were rather more exciting matters.

Last night [I wrote on Saturday, 16th February 1946] one of Mrs Jones's daughters saw a man in the next garden, that is, the second from ours. On examining the ground today I saw footprints over our air-raid shelter. Mrs Jones also had footprints in her garden.

The Man must have come over the wall of the pine-end house next-door lower down to ours. A house in Morgan St. (just by ours) was burgled last night, and Detectives warned people around to lock their doors at night.

On Wednesday, 20th March 1946, there was a truly memorable event. "Jack tried to phone [Auntie] Annie from London," I wrote, "but got the police station instead. He said he would be on the 5.0 a.m. mail train, so we went to meet him. Uncle Glyn brought the car. My mother and I walked through the silent streets to the station. I got up at 3.0 am. and stayed up."

The arrival of my Uncle Jack on home leave was really exciting: apart from everything else, I could not recall ever having got up so early. The platform at High Street Station was not quite deserted, as a few other folk had turned up to meet returning servicemen. When the train came in I rushed forward to greet a short, fair-haired young man in air force uniform – precisely the figure I had expected from the photographs he sent us. Somewhat to my surprise (for overt expressions of affection were frowned upon in those days) he took me by the shoulders and hugged me. I felt his whiskery chin on my cheek.

"Hello, boy," he said, "lovely to see you."

Then he turned to my Mother and Uncle Glyn.

"Hullo, Jack," said she.

"Hello, John," said Uncle Glyn, suavely. He always called Jack 'John' and Auntie Annie 'Ann', it was part of his genteel manner. My Mother seemed genuinely pleased at my Uncle Jack's arrival. We loaded his bags into the car and drove home. Gran had struggled out of bed to meet him as well.

During his years of absence my Uncle Jack had become something of a mystery figure. When he was posted abroad his whereabouts and activities were unknown to us, for like most servicemen he could not reveal much in his letters. The censors had a habit of cutting out bits of the texts regardless of what was written on the other side.

"Good Gordon," Sal Jones next door had said one day (she always said 'Good Gordon'), "our Jackie have sent us a letter with so much cut out it hardly holds together! Look!" She held a piece of paper with holes in it over the garden wall, for us to see.

When the rules were relaxed, however, we found that Jack was in Egypt, living under canvas, and doing a secretarial job. He sent us photographs of the pyramids, with sand, camels, and British airmen drinking beer. One day we even received a letter saying that he had found an Arab maiden called Esther, been to Crete on holiday with her, and intended to make her his wife. Everyone at No. 64 was thrown into a panic: "Oh, Gawd! An Arab?" In the Hafod such a union was unthinkable. There was talk of veils and belly dancing and worshipping Allah. In the end my Mother got Uncle Glyn, the most authoritative figure in the family, to write a strongly dissuasive letter, and everybody else, including myself, added pleas at the bottom. But a leaden silence followed, and we were left for months wondering whether a betrothal had taken place or not. For good or ill, it all blew over, so when Uncle Jack arrived at High Street Station he was still single.

During this, his first visit home after service abroad, I observed him with friendly curiosity. In most ways he was thoroughly likeable. He much resembled Gran in being kind, unpretentious, and sociable. He soon picked up with his old Swansea friends, and took obvious pleasure in their company. My Mother, perhaps the least sociable person I knew, contrasted my retiring nature with his sociability, and urged me to follow his example.

"You should be more outgoing, like Jack," she would say, flapping her elbows to indicate social contact. "Get out and meet people!"

Jack was only ten years older than myself, and during the quiet talks we had in the front bedroom I found he had the education bug as well. He had, after all, matriculated.

"I'm going to try and get a place in Bangor Teachers' College," he confided to me. "I can't go for a degree because I didn't get any Highers... Perhaps I'll do French as well. I may get into the rugby team. You don't do much sport, do you? Why not?... My gramophone? [he had bought a mechanical one, for which, he told me, he had paid sixteen shillings]. Yes, of course you can use it... I've got a wristlet watch you can have, too, if you want it. It's going."

"Oh, thank you, Jack," I said, overwhelmed. "A watch!" My Father had a spare pocket watch, acquired from Uncle Em, but he would never give it to me... And now I could listen to some of the old records from Lamb Street, perhaps even buy one or two more – I had heard wonderful recordings of Mozart on the wireless. The old gramophone in Lamb Street was a bulky piece of furniture and had long since disappeared. In terms of generosity Jack seemed to be the exact opposite of my Father, who was as mean as hell. Jack was novel in other ways, too: he used strange words and expressions such as I had never heard before: 'dobey' (washing), 'bint' (girl), 'arse bandit', 'Jesus wept', (to express exasperation), 'That's bloody rude!' and 'Fuck that for a game of marbles'.

Inevitably, his arrival in the house caused a few problems: we quarrelled once or twice over trifles, greatly frightening my Mother. He tended to come home at all hours, and upset going-to-bed arrangements. Since I had to share a double bed with him (which I hated) I could never get to sleep until he came. He always opened the window, regardless of the temperature. He might dig me in the ribs in the middle of the night to make me move over. In the end I retreated to the floor. But in the long run, I decided, having Jack around would be a good thing. His leave finished a few days later, and the best of friends, I helped him carry his suitcase to High Street Station.

The spring months and Easter holidays passed uneventfully.

We started school last Tuesday [I wrote on the 11th May]. I was sorry to go back as I was enjoying the holidays. Jack came home again on the 3rd and is going back tomorrow. I am buying stamps in school, and now have a good few. One which might be very valuable. I have nearly finished my boat and have called it the *John L. Jones*, 'L' standing for Lilian. The John is Jack. My wrist is almost healed now.

And then, on Saturday, 18th May 1946, one of the few joyful moments of my Dynevor days;

We had our concert in the Brangwyn Hall today though the old boys of the choir say that this concert is not so good as others have been. We will be broadcasting part of our next concert (Ode on St. Cecilia's Day) which is next Saturday.

I bought a programme which I will keep in memory of the occasion. That was my first concert and I will never forget the beautiful music and loud applause of the audience and the shining gilt lights gleaming in the air.

FOUR

GETTING AWAY FROM IT ALL

When we were living in Lamb Street there was never any question of us going away for a proper family holiday, in a hotel or boarding house. The most we could hope for was a visit to relatives or friends, like Gerald Peachey opposite, who came down from Scunthorpe. Gran had never even been to London. No one had enough money, and in any case Swansea itself was a seaside town. Apart from that, my Father never even tried. The trimmers allowed themselves one week's holiday a year (which was quite common at that time) and that was usually taken up by their annual 'outing' to places like to Torquay or Ilfracombe. They would, it seemed, all stay together in a cheap hotel and booze. One of my Father's pictures shows him cloth-capped with a crowd of workmates in front of a very old, open char-à-banc just before setting off. The idea of sacrificing this precious week for wife and family would, I am sure, have struck most of them as grotesque.

My Father did, however, sacrifice it once, before I was born. The cheapest thing available was a tent down Gower, the ones I saw later being round, canvass affairs with wooden floorboards. Inside there would be camp beds and a Primus stove for cooking. William Alfred took my Mother down to one of these for a few days, and she always treasured the snaps taken at the time. I do not know whether it was before or after they were married, but the pictures have a sunny glow about them: my Father, young, fit, and handsome in shirtsleeves: my Mother – young and sweet in a light summer dress. I imagine it was a holiday unspoilt by the quarrels which were to arise later.

In fact, the only outing my Father ever took me and my Mother on, before they separated, comprised a Saturday afternoon down Limeslade. This was one of the rockier bays in Gower, but fairly easy to reach. We went on one of the great maroon Mumbles trains, with two-way seats and a peculiar electric hum. The last part of the journey was on foot, and when we got there my Father and I went paddling in the rocky pools looking for crabs or anything else that could be caught. (My Mother's feet wouldn't allow her to join in.) How strange Dad looks, I thought, with his trousers rolled up over his calves, all white: I had never seen them before. The afternoon started well, without a row, but things deteriorated rapidly after tea, when my Father looked at his silver watch and declared that we would have to be getting back.

"I suppose you want to go to that old club," said my Mother, bitterly – she had rather hoped that we would be spending the evening together as well. They were soon bickering.

"Come on son," my Father said in the strange, kindly tone he always used to address me during family rows. "Get your things together, and we'll be off."

So the afternoon ended on a sour note, and my Mother and I returned to Lamb Street in the sure knowledge that my Father was having another convivial evening with his coal-trimmer friends.

* * *

If my Mother and I wanted to get away at all, regardless of what my Father did, Gower was the obvious place to go. My first real holiday there lasted a whole day and night, which was in a sense unintentional, for it was only supposed to last a day. We were already living in the Hafod, and my Auntie Mary Lizzie, (the one with St Vitus's Dance), had invited us down to her bungalow outside Murton. We went down on one of the yellow Swan buses which stopped near her field, so there was no transport problem. It was a warm, bright Sunday, and the countryside looked lovely.

When we got there we found that Auntie Mary Lizzie's bungalow was in fact a converted single-decker bus, one of the old ones with a curved wooden roof, like the school bus in Gwendraeth. It had been hauled (or perhaps driven) into a corner, hoisted onto blocks, and deprived of its wheels. I thought it was a wonderful thing to have, and wondered how she had procured it. She was waiting for us when we crossed the field – a tall, thin, white-haired woman. The frequent twitch in her jaw, that, I thought, must be the Saint Vitus's Dance. "Come in, come in," she said, smiling.

We climbed up the wooden steps and found the bus had been made into a cosy nest, with a kitchen table, chairs and a high double bed placed crosswise at the back, where the passengers used to get in. My Mother had brought bread, some spam and a pot of much treasured butter to make sandwiches: rationing was still on, and we could not expect Auntie Mary Lizzy to feed both of us. She helped herself from what we brought, and was, I recall, quite heavy on the butter. My Mother looked at me meaningfully as she spread it on.

"There's not much to do around the bungalow," said Auntie Lizzie. "But there are some nice walks."

So after the meal my Mother and I wandered around the paths and fields, gathering a few blackberries to make a tart or a jar of jam. It was a very prickly task. At one point we had to climb over a style, or sty, as I called it in those days, and as my Mother did so, very ineptly, I remembered a picture she had once shown me of her sitting on a similar structure, sylph-like, when she was young. Perhaps it was taken when she and my Father had the tent. How different, I thought, she had been in those days!

Evening drew on, and with it the prospect of going back to Swansea. We gathered our things together, thanked Auntie Mary Lizzie, and made our way to the bus stop. Despite the pleasant day my Mother was not in the best of moods.

"Your Auntie Mary Lizzie used up all my butter," she complained. "Nearly a week's ration. And all she gave me back was a lump of old marge!"

"But we had a nice day, though, didn't we?"

My Mother's indignation was not, however, assuaged. We waited at the stop for ages, but no bus appeared. Finally my Mother remembered that it was a Sunday service, and we had probably missed the last one. No hope of getting home that night! So back we went to Auntie Mary Lizzie's single-decker, where an oil lamp was already aglow.

"The last bus have gone," said my Mother, ingratiatingly. "We can't get back to Swansea. Will it be all right if we stay the night here?"

Auntie Mary Lizzy could not refuse, and stay we did, all three of us sleeping on the double bed. My Mother and I took an early morning bus back, and instead of going home I went straight to school. It was a most peculiar feeling. A good job my Mother hadn't complained about the marge, though.

* * *

My second holiday, lasting a whole week, was also in Gower. No converted bus this time, but a proper bungalow, with two rooms, a little kitchen, and electricity. My Mother and I were sharing with Gran, Auntie Annie, and her son Donald. In addition my Auntie Edith from Treboeth and her daughter Betty rented another bungalow close by. Both of my cousins were about my age, which was very convenient.

Uncle Glyn took us – the Aberdyberthi Street lot – down in his car; there was no way Gran could have got to Gower otherwise. When we arrived we found that the bungalow was not at field level, but several feet higher, behind a small sloping garden. We had great difficulty in getting Gran up the steps, but we all helped, and managed it in the end. It was clear, however, that she would be stuck inside for the whole week. Even if she got back down, there was no transport to take her anywhere. The bungalow smelt slightly of damp wood and earth. But it was all very exciting.

The atmosphere was quite relaxed because Auntie Annie was around and my Mother stopped nagging Gran. It was fun having Donald and Betty close at hand, though Donald was much more athletic than I, and kept on shinning up trees, leaving me stuck shamefully in the lower branches. And in any little dispute Betty tended to side with him, because they were first cousins, while I and she – second. But it didn't matter. We were lucky with the weather, and went down to Caswell Bay a lot: it was only half a mile or so, a pleasant walk through the woods of the valley – that is, if you could get past the patches of stink-horn without suffocating yourself. "The best thing to do is hold your nose," said Betty. I had been to Caswell many times before, but rarely arrived before early afternoon (by the time you got things ready and took two buses the day was well advanced). So seeing the bay in the morning was a new experience.

In fact, one day I got up early and wandered there by myself, coming out on the cliffs above the bay. I took a reel of cord with a fish-hook on the end in the hope of catching something, You never knew your luck. The sun was shining, the sky was cloudless, and not a soul was to be seen. There was a smell of heather in the air, and the gulls screamed overhead. For a boy from the Hafod, a magic moment indeed. I made my way down a pathway to the sand, and then along the bottom of the cliff to the water's edge.

The tide had just retreated and the rock pools were full: small watery forests with strands of dark green seaweed and white sand on the bottom. Little fish, almost transparent, darted here and there. Suddenly, I saw it: a large black crab inching its way across the bottom of the pool. I got my reel out, untangled the hook, and although I had no bait I lowered it to where I imagined the crab's mouth to be. It was walking sideways, and I was not too knowledgeable about crab anatomy. In any case, the creature was curious enough to grasp the hook with two claws.

Oh Gawd, I thought, Wonderful. I've actually caught a crab. I imagined having it fresh-boiled for supper, much to the envy of my two cousins. My Father had been very fond of crab, and I remembered him eating it in Lamb Street (though my Mother did not like the smell). Unfortunately, just as the creature broke the surface of the pool, it sensed its fate, let go, and fell back with a plop into the water. There was a flurry of sand as it hit the bottom – and then – nothing. Somehow it had escaped and was nowhere to be seen. Another disappointment in life! Although I took the line down on other occasions, I found no other. It was a lovely morning, nevertheless.

As the week went by the three of us spent most days on the sands. Donald, of course, was the most aquatic, and swam much more. I always found the water too cold for comfort, but you didn't notice it so much after the first numbing minutes. A rub-down with a rough warm towel restored the circulation afterwards, and you felt good because you had had a dip. No need for a bath either, which was good, because there wasn't one. I had brought a wooden schooner with me, one I had made myself; I dredged little channels in the sand which filled with water and I propelled the ship along them.

Returning from Caswell, though, did have its fearful moments, not least because we tended to dawdle there, and came back through the woods at dusk. Although we hardly ever met a soul, dark figures seemed to lurk in the bushes, flitting here and there; a startled bird, or a breath of wind stirring the branches would make us jump. We would peer through the gloom fearfully: would we be attacked? One evening Donald managed to lose a sandal on the beach, so we were later, and slower than ever. And there were sharp stones to contend with.

"Walking here hurts like anything," he said.

"Well, stay here, Donald," I said sympathetically. "Betty and me will go on to the bungalow and get you some shoes. You might cut your foot."

"If anything happens, shout out, and we'll find a policeman," said Betty, helpfully.

"Oh no," said Donald firmly. "We'll all go together. I'd rather have cut feet than a cut throat!"

We all thought that was very funny, and laughed like anything in the dark. We were nearly home, anyway.

★ ★ ★

My stay at the bungalow was, however, darkened by an unexpected tragedy. Since there was no one left in Aberdyberthi Street, we had had to bring the cat with us in a cardboard box. About that time we had a playful black and white kitten which I christened Admiral Benbow; the name cropped up in a story of seventeenth-century sea battles, and it stuck in my mind. Shortly before we were due to leave the bungalow I decided to feed him: but he was nowhere to be found.

"Where's Admiral Benbow?" I asked. "Anyone seen him? He hasn't got lost, has he?"

Everybody had a look around, except Gran, who was sitting on an old sofa, and couldn't move much. But she showed a lively interest in proceedings and kept on suggesting new places to look. "The'l thing's not under one of the beds, is it?" ... "Have a look in the bushes outside!" ... "Try the kitchen!" ... "Don't worry, Son, (she said to me) it'll come back before we go! Put some milk down for him!"

The mystery was solved an hour or so later, when Gran had to get up. Alas, Admiral Benbow lay flattened and dead under the cushions where she had settled: she was somewhat overweight and had not felt his slight frame when she dropped on to them. So there were recriminations and imminent tears – "Gran, how could you do it?" – but I knew that poor Gran was not to blame. I assuaged my grief by making a little grave for him in the garden. Donald and Betty were evidently of tougher metal, because they were not affected. But then, it was not their cat.

★ ★ ★

I first ventured outside Wales when I was about eleven.

"We'll be going to see your Auntie Olive and Uncle Trevor in Bristol," my Mother declared one day. "In the summer holidays. Auntie Olive have just written to say we can come for a week."

I was delighted. Bristol was another world, and I had long wanted to go there. My three Bristol cousins, Glyn, 'Little' Olive and Beryl had already been down to Swansea, staying with Auntie Kate and Auntie Annie, so I knew them well. I looked forward to going like anything.

Even getting there was an adventure. We only had one suitcase in the house, a cheap, green thing with a broken lock: my Father's posh leather one was over in Osterley Street, and he would never have lent it to us anyway. My Mother packed it the night before. On

Saturday morning, when the hour of departure came, we lugged it
down to the bus stop outside the Hafod Inn (no trolleys in those
days), but fortunately, it was not raining. When we got off the bus
outside High Street Station there was no question of getting help
there, either – there were lots of porters, but they all expected tips.
We found the train, and a compartment that had an empty window
seat facing the engine. Then there was the getting in, hoisting the
case onto the net rack, greeting other passengers, and making
ourselves comfortable. Noise, bustle, the uniformed guard, whiffs
of smoke and steam...

"How long have we got before we're off?" I asked my Mother.

There was just enough time to run down the platform and look
at the engine, a huge Great Western, probably a 2-6-4, hissing and
smelling of hot oil, with green paintwork and gleaming metal
underparts. I glanced up at the footplate: all the exciting things
were there – the throttle, reversing lever, steam brake, water gauges,
roaring furnace, and coal piled in the tender, all vastly superior to
the little colliery engines in Gwendraeth. The driver looked down
at me with a slight air, I thought, of condescension. Then back to
the compartment to join my Mother before the guard's whistle, the
engine's answering hoot, and the first shuddering movement.
Slowly we pulled out of Swansea, passing the sidings, Maliphant
Street and the old canal: they looked quite different from a moving
train window. As we chuffed through the Vale of Glamorgan I put
my head out of the window to glimpse the engine in the distance.

"Careful!" said my Mother. "You'll get soot in your eyes."

I didn't. We had to change trains at Cardiff, taking care not to get
on the wrong train and end up in Pontypridd, as Auntie Olive and
Uncle Trevor had done once before. This time we shared a
compartment with a man who knew a bit about the journey.

"After Newport we'll be going through the Severn Tunnel," he
said. "It goes under the estuary."

We hadn't done that in geography, so I thought the tunnel was
seven miles long. I wondered how long it would take us to get
through it.

"You'll have to close the window," said the man, "the smoke gets
terrible."

But there must be enough air to breathe, I thought, or everyone
would suffocate.

A few miles out of Newport the line indeed descended into a
brown sandstone cutting, and suddenly we were in the tunnel itself.
The roar of wheels reverberated throughout, while steam and sooty

air swirled through the window. The dim lamps of the compartment came on. "Close the window quick," said the man, but I needed no prompting, the smell was dreadful. I pulled on the thick leather strap which drew it up through the door frame. The light from the compartment danced on the black walls of the tunnel outside, and if you looked intently you could see, from time to time, little apertures, like fireplaces.

"They're for the workmen to stand back in when a train passes," the man explained. It must have been frightening, I thought, to have the great wheels thundering past only a few inches from your head.

"They put their caps over their faces," said the man, "so that they don't breath the smoke in."

The tunnel seemed endless, but at last we were out again into the sunshine, steaming along the southern plain of the Severn estuary. Then Bristol Meads Station, another change of train, a much smaller one this time with a tank engine, to take us down to Shirehampton.

★ ★ ★

When we got there (by now it was mid afternoon) we found my Uncle Trevor Joseph waiting to welcome us on the platform. He was a short, thick-set man with reddish hair, whom I had also seen in Swansea. The station was within walking distance of the house, and he had come to help with the case.

Slowly we made our way to No. 37 Old Quarry Road – one of a row of council houses with a gate and a little flower garden in front. Behind, as I soon found out, was another, long garden planted with vegetables. No. 37 was not nearly as impressive as No. 17 Osterley Street, but it was definitely better than Gran's: there was a third, tiny bedroom and a table-topped bath in the kitchen. Although the lav was outside, it was just opposite the kitchen door, so you could go without getting wet. There was also a back entrance at the bottom of the garden. There were plum trees, unthinkable in the Hafod, and the soil was light brown, unlike the black earth at home.

Auntie Olive and my cousins were there to greet us: the younger generation, born Bristolians, had strange, Gloucester accents. Glyn was a diminutive little boy, about two years younger than I, with a large forehead. He never seemed to do anything except go the 'pichas'. Beryl and little Olive were a few years older, a lively pair, who (I was to find) enjoyed teasing me.

It was the first chance I had to get to know the family intimately. Unlike my Father, Uncle Trevor had no social aspirations, and would probably not have known what they were, if asked. He was perfectly content to spend his life stoking a furnace at a works in Avonmouth. I never saw him in a suit, as he preferred to wear a sports jacket and flannel trousers. Most of his spare time, I was told, went on growing vegetables or playing bowls. He often went down to the local pub, the 'Ope and Anchor, but beery conviviality never had the hold on him that it did on my Father. Uncle Trevor would sometimes take Auntie Olive with him to have a short, something my Father would never even have contemplated.*

The only unusual thing Uncle Trevor had ever done, it seemed, was to serve as a cavalryman in the First World War, though mostly in the stables, and not, like my Father, at the front. I had seen pictures of him in the family albums, looking very smart in a private's uniform with puttees. He was a Hafod boy and had had little education, apart from which he seemed very thick – as though he had just been hit on the head, I thought. That suited my Auntie Olive because she was thick too. (In the Hafod my Mother would say, "Your Auntie Olive is very thick!" and laugh.) The Josephs had come to Bristol many years before when employment in Swansea was bad, and Uncle Trevor got a job at the Avonmouth spelter works. No one in the house (including Uncle Trevor himself) seemed quite sure what 'spelter' was, or what was done with it.

My Auntie Olive was the eldest of Gran's three daughters; she was a kind little woman with a flat face. My Mother once told me Gran had taken her to see a doctor at the age of four because no one could understand what she said. 'Lewis Lewis', the well-known draper's, for example, came out as 'Diddy Diddy'. Gran must have been very worried, because the cost of a visit was relatively enormous.

"Don't worry," said the doctor, after some sort of examination. "There's nothing wrong with her. She's just a bit slow. It will come."

I don't think Auntie Olive herself ever noticed anything amiss. One morning, when she and I happened to be at No. 37, alone, I asked her what two sixteens were. I must have been counting something.

"Thirty three," she said after a moment's thought.

"It's thirty two, Auntie Olive."

---

* The name of the pub, incidentally, puzzled me. Of course I knew what an anchor was, but had never heard of an ope. I imagined it was a piece of ship's machinery. "What's an ope', Uncle Trevor?" I asked one day. "Well," he answered, "You goes there and 'opes you'll get a drink."

Another pause. "I was always good at arithmetic," she responded proudly. Being only one out didn't matter.

Auntie Olive, apart from her gentle nature, had another attribute that my Mother could not match, namely, a finely shaped pair of legs and dainty feet. She bought nice stockings and elegant (though inexpensive) high-heeled shoes that my Mother could not possibly have squeezed into.

★ ★ ★

It was the first time I had lived in another family, and I found it interesting to compare their rows with ours. Auntie Olive and Uncle Trevor often had them, but they were not the bitter, on-going exchanges I had to put up with in Lamb Street and Aberdyberthi Street. They were robust, passing skirmishes to which each side had long accommodated. For example, Uncle Trevor's true earnings were a sure-fire source of dissension.

"I couldn't get them onion seeds I wanted yesterday," he might say, "you can't do much on six pounds a week."

"Six pounds?" Auntie Olive would shout immediately, "you don't get six pounds. I knows you gets over eight."

It was obviously a well-worn dispute practised many times.

"There's not much over from six pounds," Uncle Trevor would respond with a blank expression, as though she had not said anything. And the argument was over: Auntie Olive knew she could never get the true figure out of him.

Years later, when I heard Oscar Wilde's famous witticism: "He has no enemies, but is thoroughly disliked by his friends," I thought it well fitted the situation at Quarry Road. Auntie Olive and Uncle Trevor were in no sense enemies, but they went on rather disliking one another for decades. There was no question of them breaking up – Auntie Olive would have been terrified, and the thought, I am sure, never penetrated Uncle Trevor's skull. They both believed that men and women were naturally different and supposed to disagree, and that was that. Since Uncle Trevor was the only wage earner in the family and kept all five of them without a murmur, he always came out on top. Whatever he said went.

I thought that young Glyn always got the worst deal – his Father was so restrictive.

"Our Glyn can't go down to Swansea this summer," Uncle Trevor declared one day, when my Mother suggested it. "He went last summer, didn't he?" A trip to see relatives in Swansea was to be a rare thing. "No, you can't go to the pichas," Uncle Trevor might tell him. "You went twice last week, didn't you?" My Uncle had rigid ideas about what could and could not be done in his household.

* * *

In fact, I found soon after arriving, that I was not getting on very well with him – we just did not hit it off together. The first irritant, admittedly minor, was the lamb stew which he greatly relished. Auntie Olive made it from vegetables that came fresh from the garden and the allotment nearby. Uncle Trevor was then working afternoon shifts and was usually home for lunch: he preferred to eat the stew after removing his false teeth, and the slurping sound was terrible, far worse than anything Gran or Jack did in the Hafod. When I first heard it I was horrified and looked up at the ceiling in despair. I think he may have noticed: and I definitely infuriated him afterwards by taking a second piece of apple tart.

"Dad usually takes that piece of tart to work with him the next day," Beryl explained later. "He was very annoyed."

The climbing incident followed. I locked myself out one day when there was no one there, and the only way I could get back in was by putting the remains of a metal bedframe on the flat roof of the lav, and using it as a ladder to get up to the bedroom window. Uncle Trevor found out about it from a neighbour, and was wild.

"What was you doing up there then?" he asked. "Who said you could take that bedframe? I uses it to keep the cats off the tomatoes!"

Then there was the clock. Auntie Olive had a chiming clock (rather like my Father's Westminster Chime) which did not work. I decided to get it going again, believing it to be merely overwound. Auntie Olive would be delighted. One afternoon I took it up to the front bedroom, where I would not be disturbed, and tried to take it apart. The hands would have to come off, and the mechanism pulled out from the back. Unfortunately, the hands were held on by a small steel spigot which I could not extract. In the end I cut it, only to find, to my horror, that the hour hand would not come off anyway, and the mechanism still would not come out. The big hand hung loose now, as well.

"I wasn't able to mend your clock, Auntie Olive," I said apologetically. "I've left it in the cupboard upstairs." Uncle Trevor, sensing trouble, went to have a look.

"Now he's broken the sodding thing worse," he told her.

If Uncle Trevor began to dislike me there may also have been a deeper reason, an underlying resentment.

"Have you got any books anywhere, Uncle Trevor?" I asked him innocently one day. The question clearly got his hackles up.

"I don't like books," he answered curtly, "we're ordinary people here." Whereas my Father took no interest at all in education, Uncle Trevor seemed actively to disdain it. I gathered from one or two other remarks that he resented the idea of my trying my Scholarship and staying on in school – it was not something that a working class boy should do.

Poor Glyn, I thought, I'm glad I haven't got a Father like him.

Dealing with Uncle Trevor put William Alfred into a rather more favourable light, though I had to admit that Uncle Trevor had his solid virtues and was, in his dour way, much more concerned about his family.

* * *

Auntie Olive was very sociable, like Gran, and saw a lot of her neighbours. The woman next door, a tall fair-haired creature in her thirties, was always running in. She was called Sadie, and had a little daughter called Georgina. Sadie came to meet us soon after we arrived, providing me with another strange experience.

"This is my sister Lily and her son Mervyn," said Auntie Olive, when Sadie came into the kitchen. Sadie smiled and responded with a string of words that I found totally incomprehensible. It was most embarrassing, for if you couldn't understand, you couldn't answer. No one seemed to have any trouble, except me.

Little Olive looked at me and giggled.

"It's all right," she whispered in her broad Bristol, "You get used to it, Sadie's from Scotland."

Sadie naturally doted on Georgina, whom I remember as a little girl in a white dress. One day we went down to the beach at Minehead, and Auntie Olive asked her to photograph us on the sand, with Georgina playing in front. When the photograph was developed we found that everybody's head had been cut off, because Sadie wanted Georgina to be in the centre.

"Silly bitch," said Uncle Trevor, when he saw it.

Glyn and I, however, nearly brought the child to a sticky end. Sadie came in one morning and said something to Glyn. He translated.

"She wants us to take Georgina out in her pram for a bit, so that she can get on with the cleaning," he said.

There was not much else happening, so I agreed. We went next door to find the pram all ready, with Georgina sitting in it dressed in white. The walk was pretty boring, but at least Georgina caused no trouble. The district was a little hilly, and eventually we got to a brick walkway which descended steeply to a street, with a flight of steps at the bottom.

By then Glyn was telling me about one of his pichas, I thought he was holding the pram, he thought I was, but neither of us were. In a flash it was rolling down the walkway faster and faster, and quite out of control. There was hardly even time to shout: we were both terribly scared. We rushed after it, and just managed to catch it before it tumbled over the steps. Had it done so, Geogina would certainly have been thrown out and injured or concussed. We looked at one another, white and breathless.

"For Gawd's sake, don't say anything to Sadie," I said. "She'll go mad."

"You're dead right!"

Georgina was too small to understand how close she had come to disaster, and couldn't tell her Mother, anyway. So the incident was to remain for ever a deep secret. That is, until it appeared on this page.

★ ★ ★

"We'll go down to the 'Ope and Anchor for an hour this evening", Auntie Olive told my Mother one day. "Trevor said he'll take us. Little Olive and Beryl can stay with the boys."

I was horrified.

"My Mother can't go there," I said, with years of Sunday School inculcation behind me. "She doesn't drink or smoke. Ma, don't go."

My Mother smiled in a rather embarrassed way. She always said she wasn't a pubbing woman, and I was all too familiar with her tirades against my Father's habits. My cousins decided to take me in hand, for in Quarry Road the idea of not having a drink seemed daft.

"You mustn't stop your Mother having a little drink now and again, Mervyn," said Little Olive, with a beatific smile. "It won't do her no harm."

"But she doesn't go into pubs!"

"There's nothing wrong with it," Beryl urged. "Lots of people go into pubs! Jesus drank wine, didn't he? You can read about it in the Bible! As long as you don't get drunk. You won't do that, Auntie Lily, will you?" she added, turning to my Mother.

"Trevor takes me down sometimes," Auntie Olive added, "Mind, I never haves very much. But it's nice to go there."

"There, you see?" Little Olive continued. "You mustn't stop your Mother enjoying herself a bit! They won't be back late. And we'll have a lovely mushroom supper when they gets home."

I knew I had lost the battle, and off they all went, dressed in their best clothes. The mushrooms were indeed there, ready to be cooked. I had picked them that very day.

* * *

The point was that in those days Quarry Road ended in an area of field and woodland, and I had gone off that morning to explore it. The trees were rather sparse, and I found one could ramble at will. It was not long before a white-capped mushroom caught my eye, and then another, and another. They were, it appeared, quite plentiful – the same as you could get in the Hafod, though they had a slight pinkish underside that I had never noticed before. In Swansea mushrooms were dear and cost 1s 6d a quarter, so my Mother hardly bought them. I could remember my Father eating them, though, with fried bread and bacon, when we were in Lamb Street. I rushed back to Auntie Olive's, got a large saucepan, and returned to collect several pounds, a feast for everyone in the house.

When my Mother, Auntie Olive and Uncle Trevor got back from the Ope and Anchor that evening, the tiniest bit tipsy, we had a tremendous fry-up, and the air in the kitchen turned blue with the fumes. The mushrooms tasted delicious with bacon. After supper we all went to bed, and I turned in with Glyn in the front bedroom as usual. I had, it seemed, only just dropped off when I was awakened by noise in the next room – sort of groan, followed by a splashing sound. Just like someone being sick.

"For Chrisht's sake, Olive," I heard Uncle Trevor grunt (people from the Hafod always said 'Chrisht' – it was less blasphemous). "You fetched up all over the floor."

"I didn't have time to find the po," said Auntie Olive in a choked voice. "A-a-a-a" (spatter, spatter).

"Well for Gawd's sake go down to the lav," said Uncle Trevor, "so that I can get some cowing sleep. I got to go to work tomorrow." Before long, all the women were up being sick into whatever receptacles they could find – quick.

The following morning was grey, and no one wanted much breakfast.

"It was them mushrooms, Mervyn," said Auntie Olive, looking at me reproachfully with her soft brown eyes. She didn't get wild, like my Mother. "You nearly poisoned us. We could all be dead."

"They looked all right to me," I said stoutly. "Just like the ones they sell in Swansea market."

Uncle Trevor, Glyn and I were perfectly all right, and Uncle Trevor went to work as usual. But he was a tough nut.

* * *

"Don't mention anything about soot or chimneys while you're here," Little Olive to me mysteriously one day. "It might upset Mum."

"Yes, a terrible thing happened before you came up," Beryl added. "It's painful memories."

"What was that, then?"

The girls went into graphic detail. After dinner on a Sunday Auntie Olive liked to stack the dishes and settle down for a fag and a doze in front of the black kitchen range. (In the Hafod, despite my Mother's distracted habits, the dishes were always washed up straight away.)

"She was just sitting there, having a smoke," said Beryl, "when there was loud banging on the front door. Then someone pushed it open, for we don't normally lock it."

"A crowd of firemen rushed in," said Olive, "all in their uniforms and helmets."

"And with a hose" Beryl added. "They filled the whole room. 'Your chimney's on fire, missus, and you've been reported,' they said. "We've got to be sure it's out!' "

"Mum didn't know where to turn. They said it was dangerous, and poked the hose up the chimney. The mess was terrible."

"Where was Uncle Trevor?"

"He was upstairs having his Sunday afternoon nap. He came down looking as black as hell."

"The mess wasn't the worst of it," said Olive. "The firemen said Mum and Dad would have to pay a big fine for endangering the house and getting the fire brigade out. They said Mum could have burnt the whole terrace down. When they had gone, Dad played hell with her, because it was his money, anyway."

"They should have had it cleaned before," said Beryl, "It was both their faults."

"Where were you, then?" I asked.

"Out doing the allotment with Glyn, weren't we?" she said, and looked questioningly at her sister.

* * *

"There's lots of things to see in Bristol," someone had said, a day or so after we had arrived. "The Clifton Suspension Bridge, the Severn Bore and the Zoo."

I had heard of the Clifton Suspension Bridge, and even seen a picture of it gracefully spanning Clifton Gorge, but the 'bore' was a new one on me. Was it a hole, a wild pig, or a tedious talker?

"What's the Severn Bore?" I asked.

"It's a great big wave that runs up the Severn at certain times," Olive answered dramatically. "If you want to see it, you've got to know when. Dad will show you, if you want to!"

A day or two later Uncle Trevor dutifully took us to see both the Bridge and the Bore: of the two, I found the Bridge most interesting, especially when they told me that it was a favourite spot for suicides. Gawd, I thought, just imagine jumping off that! The Bore turned out to be quite a little wave, much smaller than I expected. But I did not say anything to Uncle Trevor, so as not to disappoint him. He was very proud of the Bristol sights.

We did not have a zoo in Swansea, apart from a couple of caged foxes in Cwmdonkin Park, which stank like anything. "The Zoo in Bristol is a proper one," Little Olive boasted, "with an aviary for birds, a reptile house and all sorts of wild animals... But," she continued after a pause, "the main thing is Alfred the gorilla. Everyone goes to see him."

When we arrived I found that Alfred lived in an enormous green cage, with some hefty boughs to hang on. The area in front of it was thronged with visitors. Alfred – a great, hairy, creature with a sharply receding forehead and restless eyes – was perched high in one corner. He looked fearful, but was, I suppose, docile enough, tamed by years of good living and admiring glances. The thing that struck me most, however, was his enormous posterior, which he displayed with disconcerting abandon. Auntie Olive, who regarded herself as a respectable working class woman, was hugely embarrassed.

"I think he likes showing it," she said apologetically. "The same thing happened when your Uncle Glyn and Auntie Annie brought Donald up a few years ago."

The girls looked at one another meaningfully.

"What happened?" asked my Mother.

1. Gran manages a smile in the backyard of No. 64 Aberdyberthi Street

2. Working class respectability: Gamma and my Grandfather at Osterley Street

3. Coaltrimmers at the dockside, my Father is second from the right.

4. Mervyn, the little bus conductor –
with Dad at Osterley Street

5. My Mother and Father, the only
time they were photographed
together, when they were married

Clockwise from top left. 6. Early days: my Mother outside the tent in Gower at the time of her marriage. 7. Mother poses on a stile in Gower. 8. Just out of hospital: my Mother and I in the garden of No. 64. 9. The only photograph of my Mother and Jack

11. My Mother as a graceful young woman

10. My Father as a handsome young man

13. My half-sister Doreen as a bridesmaid

12. Jack on the Nile

Clockwise from top left. 14. Auntie Beatrice and one of her daughters. 15. Auntie Kate, her husband Uncle Gilbert, Auntie Annie and, reclining in front, Uncle Glyn. 16. Uncle Trevor ready for action. 17. Auntie Olive

Clockwise from top left. 18. Auntie Enid with Donnie and Gordon (my second cousins) in Aberdyberthi Street. 19. In Bristol: left, my cousin Donald and, right, my cousin Glyn, with an unknown friend. 20. Michael has a quiet read at Hill House. 21. 'Auntie' Elsie and my friend John Lewis, outside Elsie's little shop.

Two faces of war. 22. Swansea bombed flat. 23. Street party outside No. 64
(second doorway from right, with the peaked wooden frame). Marge Stanbury
is second from right, leaning forward.

"You knows how prim and proper Glyn is," said Auntie Olive. "Donald was a lovely little boy then, with curly hair and a white shirt. Glyn lifted him up and put him on his shoulder so that he could see better." Her voice sank lower. "When Donald saw the gorilla he shouted, 'Oh, Dad, look at his A-S-S-H-O-L-E!' at the top of his voice."

"With a Welsh accent!" one of my cousins added.

"Everybody heard, and Glyn was mortified. He got Donald down pretty quick. No one knew where the boy got that word from."

I could well understand my cousin's astonishment; I had never seen anything like it, either.

In fact I thought about the zoo on the train, a few days later, when my Mother and I were returning to Swansea. The journey back was much less exciting, because there was no adventure at the end, only Gran and life in the Hafod. Yet how strange it was that a gorilla's bum should be among the impressions that I brought back from my holiday in England. Almost beyond mention, of course, except to friends. If anyone asked, I would tell them about the Clifton Suspension Bridge and the Severn Bore, with only a brief mention of the great ape. Years later I heard that Alfred's mountainous corpse, presumably all of it, had been stuffed for posterity, and in fact it can be seen to this day at Bristol Museum.

* * *

My holidays in Gower and Bristol, however, were to be followed by a sojourn of quite a different order. One of my great pleasures, as I have mentioned, was cycling, usually alone. On light evenings and at weekends, weather permitting, I would swing off along the beautiful Gower coast, or through the hills and valleys of the Swansea hinterland. The freedom was exhilarating, and it allowed me to get away from the tensions of No. 64. There were few sounds dearer to my ear than the hum of the ratchet on the back axle. My bicycle, formerly Jack's, lacked the refinements of the age – there was no three-speed gear, hub dynamo or speedometer – but it was a great advance on the squat, solid-tyred vehicle I had in Lamb Street. I never allowed my frequent doubts about the reliability of the cable brakes to deter me from speeding.

One afternoon in 1946, while riding near Felindre, I put on a burst of speed. There was loose gravel on the road, and my bicycle went in to an uncontrollable skid. I fell and landed heavily on my left hip, with the frame on top of me. Fortunately, there seemed to be no great injury. It took me only a minute or two to extract myself and wipe my grazed knees. The bicycle was undamaged, and after a short rest I was on my way again.

Soon afterwards, however, my Mother started peering at me on odd occasions. One day she took me to town shopping, and lagged behind, evidently to observe my gait. After that events moved rapidly. On the 30th May, shortly after the school choir broadcast its concert, I wrote in my diary that my left leg was 'bad'. The following Saturday was the official Victory Day: "There have been big parades in London and Cardiff," I noted, "although it is very quiet here, with only dancing by the Civic Centre. My leg is still bad, and I have been to see a doctor about it."

By then I had developed a constant limp. A series of medical examinations followed. "My Mother had the result of the X-Ray yesterday," I noted on the 18th July. "The film showed that my left hip-joint is not forming properly and I suppose I'll have to go and have treatment for it. I hope I won't have to go into hospital... I had the result of my exams [at school] today. I surprised everyone (including myself) in coming first."

My fourteenth birthday fell just a week later. I decided to continue my diary in the best French I could manage.

> Aujourdhi c'est ma jour de naissance, et j'ai reçu beaucoup de cadeaux....
>   Ce soir j'inviterai deux ami et mon cousin Donald avoir thé avec moi. Demain matin je dois aller (avec ma mere) au authopeadic clinic. Peut-être je devrai aller a l'hôpital.
>   Mon école finissait demain. Jean [Jack] reviendra a sa maison pour toujours aujourdhui".

> [Today is my birthday, and I got a lot of presents...
>   This evening I will invite two friends and my cousin Donald to have tea with me. Tomorrow morning I have to go with my Mother to the orthopaedic clinic. Perhaps I will have to go into hospital.
>   My school finishes tomorrow. Jean (Jack) will return home for good today.]

What happened after that is quite another matter. But before I pass on to it I shall relate what was going on between my estranged parents, and around them.

FIVE

GOINGS ON

My Father had much to gain by living in St. Thomas, apart from the extra comforts. He took no pleasure in my Mother's company, Osterley Street was much nearer his work, and a bachelor existence, with all its free evenings, still attracted him. He was fully thirty seven when he got married, anyway. The break with my Mother was at first complete, but as I have mentioned, she soon re-established contact, albeit acerbic, by letter. The consequences of having separated parents affected my weekly round, for my Mother would often send me over to Osterley Street, usually on a Sunday, as a go-between. On my return she would question me in great detail about what I had seen and heard.

During these visits my Father, of course, told me nothing about his emotional life, but curiously enough he shared my interest in recording events, and for three years (1942, 1943, and 1944) made brief notes in little pocket books. He would comment (sometimes in almost coded language) on his activities, and express the occasional heartfelt desire or dislike. No letter he ever wrote to me or my Mother has survived: but he seems to have kept all of the thirty or so which she sent him. Perhaps he hoped that one day they could be used as "evidence" against her, though how, he surely could not have known. In any case, the letters and notes were passed to me many years later, and (together with fragmented images in my memory) allow me to tell the story of my parents' continuing 'romance'. At the time, naturally, I had no idea what was being written on either side.

At first my Mother hoped that my Father would give me money when I went to see him, but I never got an extra penny. Yet as a good coal-trimmer, he was still giving other people presents he could ill afford, just to impress them.

Mervyn will be coming over to see you tomorrow (Thursday) [My Mother wrote on New Years' Eve, December, 1941]. Let me appeal to you to help the child in a more practical way. You can write pages of kisses to him but they dont mean a thing when accompanied by a starvation 10 shillings. If you love him as you say you do, show it in a practical way. Otherwise cut it all out, it is hypocrisy. His knees

are freezing because his coat does not cover them. A new coat for
your son would not cost as much as it did for your niece.
L. Matthews

The black market food my Father was getting from the dock was
another thorny matter. My Mother greatly envied this facility, but
could not match it – we were simply too poor.

> It is a great pity [she wrote on the 2nd January, 1942] that you have
> nothing better to do than brag to this child about the quantity of
> black market butter you are able to obtain. If you or your mother
> had any principle the boy should have a share of it rather than have
> to manage on two ounces... "Starvers of little children" is a well
> earned title for both of you. It is a damn shame that you both are
> not exposed. You are not allowing my little boy sufficient to buy
> him food and clothes, but what odds for him as long as you two can
> grease your old guts.
> L.M.

On the evening of the 3rd January my Father commented in his
diary: "Letter from her [he rarely used my Mother's Christian
name], no sense as usual, out late, Snooker at the Club." His notes
showed, however, that he greatly looked forward greatly to my visits.
"We had a lovely day together", he noted on one occasion, and any
failure on my part to write or appear on a Sunday was registered
with regret. "No letter from Mervyn today," he wrote on the 10th
January. "She is stopping him from writing. But God is good and he
knows who is to blame and 'I will repay'." The bitterness in my
Mother's letters was matched on his side, too: "Off all day, and went
to the Rialto Cinema. Alone all night, curses on my fool marriage,
oh, to have had more sense. I want to be so happy, the lonlyness is
getting me down.... Tired of the worry and my boy, not having seen
him adds to my wretchedness. Maybe I will see him tomorrow."

His affection for me, however, never induced a hint of generosity, nor any concern for my schooling. Never once did he ask me,
for example, what marks I was getting. Despite the free time on his
hands he developed no cultural interests whatever: nothing could
override the club, the pubs, the picture houses – and one other
activity I shall come to in a moment. His commitment to the lowly
pastimes of a Swansea trimmer was total.

He was much troubled by financial problems. The coal trade had
been largely ruined by the war, and his shifts, or 'turns' as he called
them, became ever more sporadic. "V.Q. [Very Quiet] on the dock"

was a recurring entry. He often complained of the cold; out in all weathers, he tended to fall ill. In the circumstances Gamma became the lynch-pin of his existence. "Busier, wet through to the skin", he wrote on the 19th January. "Mother is marvellous to dry clothes so well and ready to wear. Will be working all night. Got home for food, so O.K. Bitter cold on deck. I have a nasty cold, and mam has. But how she looks after me. I dont know what I'll do without her"... "Such bad news of the war," he wrote three days later. "Seriously thinking of joining up. I wonder how my boy is."

The Labour Club loomed so large in my Father's life that I became rather curious to see it, and indeed once ventured inside, looking for him. A surprise awaited me. I found a dark cavern-like hall with black-faced coal-trimmers in their working clothes, some sitting on benches against the walls, others drinking beer or playing billiards. It was all so drab and depressing, not at all as I had imagined; I had expected something much more stylish, to match my Father's gold chain and suits. And though I saw nothing of it on that brief occasion, there was a rough element there, too. "Bother in the club, argument", wrote my Father on the 7th June, 1944. "And yet again" he added the next day. "Stood with back to wall and fought it out".

In fact Willie Matthews was much liked and enjoyed some authority in that grimy world. He was in charge of the boozy sports teams for two years (skittles and darts), and ran the Comrades' Sick Club for ten, being eventually rewarded with the Westminster Chime clock. He kept the appointments registers meticulously, writing in a neat and fluent hand. At one point, later on, the duties got too much for him, and he tendered his resignation. "Your letter requesting the Committee to accept your resignation," wrote Glyn Charles, the acting secretary on 14th January 1944, "was duly read at last Tuesday's meeting. However, I am pleased to say, your resignation was not accepted, as it is felt that you are too good a man to lose, having regard to your valuable service on the Committee in the past. I am directed by the Committee, in passing this information to you, to express the hope that you will be present at the next Committee Meeting."

* * *

As the months went by, visiting Osterley Street became a regular activity for me. My path thither on a Sunday morning lay through some mouldering, but historic parts of the town. Down the Strand, with its row of working-class, terraced houses, past Kramsky's evil-smelling domain: past the sloping Pottery Street, where Gamma had lived many years before; under the cavernous railway bridges which supported the lines into High Street Station; across a derelict area with a cobbled road, over the swivel bridge at the end of the North Dock (where you could still see flat-fish swimming in the water); past a small boat-building yard, where they had been working on the same wooden launch for years; on to the little tar manufactory, where, on week-days, they would sell you half a gallon, warm, to take home; and finally, over the bridge at the mouth of the River Tawe, with its criss-cross girders and railway line. St. Thomas began, for me at any rate, with the huddle of sailors' pubs at the dock entrance on the other side. When I got to the town bridge I knew there was no longer any chance of my being stopped and threatened by the gangs of boys who often roamed the Strand. But in any case Sunday morning was a good time to go, as they were rarely to be seen.

I would arrive at Osterley Street shortly before lunch. It was one of the steepest streets in Swansea and Gamma's was towards the top. Inside, past the red glass door, my Father had painted the passage walls a sombre mauve, probably stolen, as usual, from some tramp-steamer in the dock. The front parlour was quite expensively furnished: Edwardian chairs, a marble fireplace with a mirrored whatnot above it, an occasional table and a piano, which (unlike the one in Aberdyberthi Street) had retained its brass candle-sticks. The walls of the middle room were adorned by two great oil landscapes in heavy gilt frames. In one corner there was a cupboard filled with story books, mostly for children, which, I was sure, no one had read for decades.

Beyond was a large kitchen which also served as the living room. It had the usual big, black-leaded grate, and a high mantelpiece with a brass shield and candlesticks, all ashine with wifely endeavour. A dresser, my late grandfather's wooden armchair, a big kitchen table, and a springless old sofa completed the furnishings. There was a dark pantry where dominoes, tins of drafts, a ringboard and other interesting things were kept. It had a warm, mysterious smell of its own. But even this was not all. A narrow door led from the kitchen into yet another room – a stone-built scullery with a table-topped bath, a copper for boiling clothes, and an enormous cast-iron mangle with cogs, rollers and a handle which I loved to turn. Upstairs were three bedrooms (one with two windows) and a large landing.

All of this represented a degree of opulence far beyond anything I knew in Lamb Street or Aberdyberthi Street. Even my Mother referred to it with a sort of reluctant reverence. The fact that the household had also produced my redoubtable Aunties Beatrice and Ethel only added to its aura. Despite the welcome I received there, I never felt at home. I had no trouble with the table manners (about the only thing my Father ever taught me) but I never felt I could do as I liked, as in Gran's. The Osterley Street house had a kind of order, or pretension, that put me off.

My Father was hugely proud of it, but even at my age I sensed a strange discrepancy in his attitudes. If he enjoyed these things at home, why had he been content to live in so small a house without hot water in Lamb Street? Why had he not tried to make things better for my Mother and me? The answer was clear: he was too concerned with drinking and having 'a good night out'.

Just as Aberdyberthi Street was Gran, so Osterley Street was Gamma. Anyone less like Gran it would be difficult to imagine. Small, dapper, bespectacled, Gamma was ever on the move, cooking, washing and tidying. You would never find her sipping glasses of beer, gossiping with neighbours, or talking about 'the working man'. As far as I could see no one ever dropped in to see her. My Mother naturally regarded Gamma as a rival for my Father's affection, and had little but malicious comment for her. The fact that Gamma had once worked as a servant, and lived in Pottery Street, was a telling point in the perpetual family rows. Yet my Mother was unfair, for despite an occasional glint of steeliness (which Gran completely lacked) Gamma was a lovely person. I never, for instance, heard her make a single negative remark about anyone on my Mother's side of the family, and she showed me only warm affection. True, she lacked schooling: but she was quick-witted – and the only member of the family who still spoke Welsh.

I would get to the house to find her busy cooking the dinner at the kitchen fire. There was no gas stove – Gamma claimed that her oven grate was excellent, and she needed nothing more.

"Hullo stranger, we've been waiting for you!" she would say. "Half the dinner was wasted last week, you didn't come! There's no one else to eat it."

My Father would be sitting at the kitchen table, next to the wireless. He always smiled when I came in, though a morning spent 'in committee' at the Club would probably have ensured a good mood anyway. The roast meat and vegetables (not quite as nice as I got in the Hafod) were soon on the table, to be followed by rice pudding.

Afterwards, as Gamma washed up, my Father would observe a ritual which never varied. He would spread a newspaper on the table, and invite me to join him in crumbling the contents of two packets of Frankinson and Moore's compressed tobacco. When we had a pile of loose shag in front of us he would produce a little cigarette machine with a rubber roller, and some cigarette paper. He would then, slowly and deliberately, roll a great number of the thinnest cigarettes I had ever seen and load them into his old leather cigarette case. After that he would pull out the Sunday newspaper from the wireless stand and check his football pools to see whether he had at last struck lucky. In all the years he did them he had, I believe, only one small win. Then, with these hebdomadal tasks completed: "I'm off to bed for a rest, now son," he would say, and retire upstairs for a couple of hours, leaving me with an awful void to fill until tea time. Gamma would doze in the kitchen.

In fact Sunday afternoon in Osterley Street, with my Father abed, was one of the most boring things in my whole life – even worse, in a way, than school. The Westminster Chime would tick impassively on the middle room mantelpiece. The ill-fitting window frame in the middle room admitted wind with an eerie whistle I never heard anywhere else. The fire in the kitchen, no longer needed for cooking, would die back a little. The old book cupboard, it is true, could be explored again, but its contents were mostly for the children of a past generation who liked scouts and Red Indians (which I did not). No pirate or sea stories there. The only relief from boredom was to be found in the tool shed at the bottom of the garden, where I could tinker about a bit, that is, if the weather was not too cold. There was a big vice, and an assortment of wooden planes which I greatly coveted, though my Father would not let me use them, for fear of blunting the blades. He would not give me one, either.

Things would come alive again only around five o'clock. My Father would come downstairs dressed in his best suit, ready for his tea, a walk with me, perhaps, and then the inevitable evening at the Labour Club. Gamma would set the tea table, complete with milk-jug and slop basin, both unknown in Aberdyberthi Street. A freshly-baked apple tart would appear from the oven, all of which meant that the end of the visit was nigh. After tea I would leave, either alone or with my Father, not a word having been uttered about my Mother or life in the Hafod. Such topics were taboo.

* * *

The criticisms which my Mother directed at Osterley Street stopped early in January, 1942, and a period of quiescence ensued. But in the spring of that year she sensed a new (or rather, renewed) cause for concern. The tone of her letters changed.

> Please Billie [she wrote on 22 April], dont make a point of mention-ing 'other engagements' to Mervyn as you did in yesterday's letter. I know you well enough to understand what you mean to convey. Mervyn will soon be old enough to realise it also.

The point was my Father had returned to a past love, if that is the right word, and my Mother had found out about it. In the years before he got married he developed a fondness for a woman called Ada Dyer who lived nearby in Danygraig Road. Ada (I was told many years later) was a 'big piece' employed as a labourer at Bald-win's Tinplate Works. She was apparently loud-mouthed and a sort of shop steward with it. She was unmarried and a 'good timer', just like my Father, though people I met years later spoke well of her. Cryptic comments in his pocket books showed that Ada was providing a weekly intimate service in various local parks.

"I could not be at the usual at 7 o'clock," he noted on Wednes-day 21st January, 1942. "I miss it, though only once a week". "Worked 6 to 2 pm," he wrote a week later. "Naughty boy. Met the usual and did it proper." Wednesday evidently became fixed for regular assignations, for several subsequent entries contained guarded comment on the levels of satisfaction achieved. "Good cheap night, but did not function with A. Still carrying it all..."

His feelings towards my Mother were still negative, but strangely enough he had not finally rejected the idea of returning to her. "I feel in myself she wants me," he wrote on Saturday, 14th February. "What am I to do. I detest her, yet my boy wants a Father to look after him. She can't. I'll bet she has missed me." And on 10th March: "Its her birthday. What she has done to me – not a word or a card will she get from me."

Yet human nature is a strange thing, and by early June 1942 feel-ings on both sides had softened enough for my Mother, despite all her misgivings, to arrange some meetings. On the 8th my Father got a letter from her saying she wanted to see him. He wrote what was evidently a nasty reply, but this only provoked another request.

> Dear Billie, I still feel that I should like to talk to you. I should like to see you alone, without Mervyn. I do not want him to hear too much. For that reason, Thursday 25th June 1942 would suit me best.

You blame me and I blame you. I blame you in as much as you had no interest in anybody or anything other than pubs and clubs... You ask me what happiness I gave you. Let me ask you what happiness did you give me? None whatever. Plenty of hard work for any coal trimmer's wife, washing, cooking, cleaning, ironing, knitting, sewing. And what at the end of it – nothing but a bare existence. Seldom 1 shilling turning to go to the pictures ... I realise that I have Mervyn's future to think of. I do not want him to know any more of our troubles than he already knows....

     L.

It seems from my Father's notes that she did indeed turn up at the Park that evening. It must have been a sad meeting. "Saw her at Ravenhill," he wrote afterwards. "Wants to go out with me. I have suffered enough. Nothing doing."

My Mother, however, was undaunted, and went on sending him notes. She also appealed to his paternal feelings, and revealed that she was trying to get us all back together under the same roof. A hapless council official by the name of Miss Jones was involved.

Dear Billie, [she wrote on the 26th August, 1942]
I wrote Miss Jones last week asking about a Corporation house but of course it might be years before we get a house at Maesteg. There are dozens of vacant houses about St. Thomas so why not try and get one rather than wait indefinitely... I have decided however that I shall hang on for a few weeks longer and in the meantime see a few councillors in the hope of getting a Corporation house. If at the end of another month or 6 weeks there is no hope of a house for us, Mervyn and I will come over and live with you at Osterley Street...

After that hopelessly impractical proposal, she continued:

I thought it best to let you know that Mervyn still has a very heavy rash. I don't know whether he will be fit enough for me to go to work tomorrow. It is when Mervyn is not well and I have to leave him first thing in the morning to be looked after by my Mother who can only drag herself about the house, that I feel it is full time you did something in the matter... Mervyn wishes me to tell his Daddy that he hopes to see him on Wednesday and that if you have found a fountain pen to bring it for him.
Love, Lil.

So the evening meetings went on, either in one of the parks, or at a picture house, with me participating. My Mother evidently thought my presence might soften my Father a bit, while he was afraid that if he did not show some flexibility my Mother would stop me seeing him altogether. Never once did he take us to a pub. He would appear in his usual rakish dress, and my Mother tried to doll herself up as well, but she looked frumpish whatever she put on, and her poor feet banished any hope of elegant deportment. If a park were chosen for the evening, a sort of coyness would descend on them, and nothing very much would be said. I would fall back and let them talk together. When the moment came for goodnight kisses, I would be hugely embarrassed and pretend not to notice.

In September my Mother took the extraordinary step of going over to see her mother-in-law to ask if we could move in. Gamma it appears, gave her the impression that she favoured the idea; but of course it never came to anything and before long my Mother resumed her recriminations and warnings. She wrote on the 20th

> Dear Billie
> If you honestly feel that you want to make a home you can drop me a card stating which time you intend going [to the housing office]. If not, I am quite prepared to let matters take their course through the court. I know I would get a square deal in a Court of Justice.
> Sincerely yours, Lil.

My Father had no intention of going near the housing office, but despite the apparently unbridgeable differences my Mother continued meeting him throughout the winter. In January 1943, no doubt as a result of a New Year Resolution, my Father re-started his diary notes, and these showed that his attitude towards my Mother was still ambivalent.

"Thinking of the great mistake I made in marrying L.J.," he wrote, "how I have paid for it. Yet sometimes I want her back. Oh, if she would only change." And again: "Sometimes I detest her, yet once I loved her as she did me. I am wondering if she appealed would I go back. No, she would have to come to me." In mid-February, 1943, the town was again badly bombed. "A lot of damage, too. Very lucky I didn't walk into it," my Father wrote on the 16th.

Whether the bombing (or likelihood of it) rendered the walks unsafe, I cannot say; but soon afterwards my parents again stopped seeing one another again.

★ ★ ★

Meanwhile, Auntie Beatrice was keeping an eye on things, as she had done in our Lamb Street days. Although they were not on speaking terms, my Mother drew what advantage she could from her sister-in-law's interest. Auntie Beatrice was once reported to have said that William Alfred was 'living in sin', and my Mother would quote this triumphantly whenever an occasion arose.

One day Auntie Beatrice somehow got in touch with me (I have forgotten how) and invited me to tea at her house in Cockett. I was puzzled, but decided to go. What did she want? What could she do?

She lived in a row of little semi-detached houses, with a neat, well-kept garden in front and a narrow front door. I rang the doorbell and she appeared almost immediately. She was dressed in a spotless linen apron, rather like Gamma's, though Auntie Beatrice was a much bigger woman. She greeted me with a smile, behind which I thought I detected a slight hint of tears. She was always like that.

"Come in son, lovely to see you. We'll have a nice cup of tea in a minute. Your Uncle Charlie will be home soon. There was something he wanted to tell you."

"Oh, really. Where's he working now, Auntie Beatrice?"

"He's in business in Llanelly," she replied. (I knew, from my Mother's caustic comment, that he was only a sales assistant in a furniture shop: but Auntie Beatrice always said he was 'in business' – it sounded better.)

"And how is your Spiritualist work going?"

"Very well, Son," she replied. "Very well. I still does the services with your Uncle Charlie. He knows all the theology, and gives the sermon. I'm the medium." She grasped the narrow bridge of her nose with a thumb and forefinger, and bowed her head for a moment. "Take your coat off, then."

Just then the front door latch clicked, and in walked Uncle Charlie, a friendly, fat little man in a dark suit, in other words, just the sort of person you expect to find in a furniture shop in Llanelly. I had met him before, possibly at Gamma's, when I was small. As soon as I heard his voice I remembered that he had a mixed English and Welsh accent and was careless with his aitches. I wonder what sort of sermons he preaches? I thought.

"Ullo, Mervyn," Uncle Charlie exclaimed. "There's nice of you to come, isn't it? My goodness, you've grown since I last saw you. 'Ow many years ago was that, then?"

"Your tea won't take long, Charlie," said Auntie Beatrice, "I'll go and do it."

Uncle Charlie glanced cautiously at the empty doorway after she left, and I had the feeling that he was going to reveal why they had asked me up.

"Do you 'ave much free time now, Son?" he asked.

"Not very much, Uncle Charlie," I said.

"You're good with your 'ands, though, aren't you?"

Now I had some inkling of what was coming: information about my handiman activities in Aberdyberthi Street had evidently filtered through.

"Well, not all that good, Uncle Charlie," I said defensively. "I have a lot on in school."

Uncle Charlie's face fell. "Your Auntie Beatrice and me was going to ask you if you could help us paper the front bedroom. We can't reach up, see."

"Sorry, I wouldn't be able to help," I said firmly. "I can't paper, anyway." Whatever next, I thought. There was a moment's awkward silence.

"There was something else I wanted to tell you as well," said Uncle Charlie, changing gear. "Your Auntie Beatrice 'aven't been very well recently. There's been a big upset".

Oh, my Gawd, I thought, she's been in the loony bin again. But I was wrong.

"Oh, really?"

"With your Father, Son. Last week she went over to Osterley Street to 'ave a word with him, when she sees things is wrong, she tries to put them right."

"I know that. What happened, then?"

"Your Father didn't understand 'er, and lost 'is temper," said Uncle Charlie. "There was words in the passage behind the red glass door. 'E grabbed 'old of 'er harm like that [Uncle Charlie grabbed mine] and pushed 'er out onto the steps. She was weeping, poor thing."

It seemed clear that my Auntie Beatrice had provoked a scuffle – or something like one – with her brother, and my Uncle Emrys had not been there to calm things down. But my Father had not mentioned it to me, and there was nothing I could say.

"What are you telling the boy?" Auntie Beatrice called out from the kitchen, for she had clearly heard every word. "William Alfred was a bit annoyed, that's all."

"Well, I think it only right that Mervyn should know what 'is Father done to you," said Uncle Charlie expressively. "She's a lovely woman, idn she?" he added to me, in a low voice. "Trying to play it down! And she does a nice'l service, too." Then aloud: "You was very upset, dear, and your harm was all black and blue. I made you go to the doctor, didn't I? You didn't want too, but I was hadamant. Hadamant!"

At that moment Auntie Beatrice reappeared with the cups of tea on a tray, and set them out on the table – all very neat, not a bit like Aberdyberthi Street. The conversation became rather desultory – everything that was important had been said. Finally Auntie Beatrice offered to foretell my future from the tea leaves in my cup, and did so, while Uncle Charlie looked on with obvious reverence. I had never had my future foretold before, but everything she said was so vague as to be almost meaningless, with dark figures and open doors, etc.

"Now remember everything I told you, Son," she said as she finished. "It will all come true."

"Your Auntie is a very talented medium," said Uncle Charlie. "She's very good at unmasking imposters, too. She caught someone faking spirits with shadows and a lamp a few months ago. She's got to put things right, see."

Well, I thought in the bus going back, that was all a bit pointless, wasn't it! I decided not to tell my Mother about the visit, unless she found out and questioned me. It wouldn't do any good.

* * *

In March, 1943 my Father's miserable existence was made even more miserable by two bombshells of an emotional character. The first took the form of a summons to appear at the police court to answer his wife's complaint of "wilful neglect to provide reasonable maintenance" following his desertion of her on the 27th June, 1941. My Father, I learned, was greatly upset about a public appearance in such circumstances. "He never thought your Mother would take him to court," Auntie Beatrice said later. The case was heard on the 13th April, and the court issued a maintenance order for £2.10s a week, that is, more than twice as much as my Father had been sending us. The order was to remain in force until I reached the age of sixteen. In fact, my Father's tax papers show he was then earning over £400 a year, so the imposition was not all that onerous. My Mother had not wanted to take the matter so far, and a letter which she (most unusually) sent to Gamma afterwards had a ring of sincerity about it.

Dear Mrs. Matthews

I feel I must follow the dictates of my heart and write and tell you that what I wanted was a home with Billie not a final separation. I could not go on any longer living as I was. I have heard a lot about Billie since we have been living apart and I have received anonymous letters which have hurt me more than I can tell but I had resolved that what was past, was past, and that we would live for the future and for our boy. Could you help me? Could Mervyn and I come there to you until Billie can make a home for us? I loved him when I married him and I still love him and I love his boy. He is so much like him in every way.

Sincerely yours, Lil.

If my Mother acted more in desperation than in anger, my Father was horrified not only by the summons, but also by his new financial burden. The fact that the order was designed to help a son whom he professed to love did not seem to mollify him at all. "I cursed the order," he wrote in his pocket book on the 18th May. And naturally enough my Mother's appeal to Gamma brought no change in the situation.

The second bombshell was not so much new as delayed-action, so to speak. On the 3rd of the month (as attested by the postmark) an unknown hand dropped a letter into a Swansea post box, and the following day it reached Gamma at No. 17.

If your son Willie Mathews would like to know that is wife goes along Port Tenant nearly every morning 9 clock in a motor car [my Mother had indeed begun a new job over at Llandarcy, and used some sort of office transport] but since he have been parted from is wife and was seen back with Ada Dyer people all says it is her he would have married if it wasnt for you. She knew him sinse he was a telegram boy and went to all the baldwins picknics with him people all knows you never wanted him to get married and that is how they blames you for all the trouble but you will have a lot to answer for now that he got a daughter [two words crossed out] to keep and a wife and child who he don't live with.

The letter did not visibly affect Gamma, and I, of course, was unaware of its existence. But as I was to learn many years later, a long story lay behind it. On the 9th March, 1931, just under a year before my Mother and Father got married, Ada Dyer gave birth to a girl whom she named Doreen. At that time Ada shared a house in Danygraig Road – then called Danygraig Terrace – with two male relatives; Doreen's birth certificate (a copy of which I subsequently obtained) lacked an entry for the father. On the 29th March, barely three weeks after the birth, William Alfred had written one of his dreadful poems on the back of a flattering photograph of himself, though the female to whom it was directed was unnamed. I suspect it was intended for my Mother, but there is no way of knowing: in any case, it was either not sent, or was returned.

> Dear little girl you seem more to me,
> You brought to my heart a sweet melody.
> Here on this card, I wear not a smile
> But beneath the mask is a heart worth while.
>
> Living and longing for you alone.
> You taught me in kindness my ways to atone.
> In a haven of love, let us bury the past
> And live in the rapture due us at last.

As one of my aunties told me many years later, my Father always denied intimacy with Ada, and told Gamma that he was taking on the mantle of paternity to help an old friend. Ada's lifestyle would, in any case, have facilitated numerous penetrations into her person. As it was, my Father, on being shown the note, could only have read it in the sad realisation that his putative fatherhood was not only known to his Mother, but also the subject of malevolent observation by others. In fact a lot of people must have been aware of it – my Mother certainly was. Gamma was not a gossipy person, and may not have known – before she received the note. The writer's aim was to bring her up to date, eleven years after the event, and possibly stir up trouble between her and her beloved William Alfred.

My Father's papers yielded, if not proof, then a strong likelihood that he had fathered another child. He retained two photographs of a young girl, one inscribed in his hand "Doreen, June 10th 1942, age 11", and the other "age 15 – 1946." He would hardly have kept them and noted the dates unless Doreen was relevant to his personal life. Yet to judge from his diary notes, she played little or no part in it – at least a 'D.' was only mentioned once, whereas 'M.' came up frequently. His notes were strictly confidential, and had he been seeing Doreen there is no reason why he should not have mentioned it. Another family member on my Father's side later revealed that he paid maintenance for her until she was fourteen; if so, this may partly have explained his meanness towards my

Mother and me.

In any case, Doreen went to Danygraig school and as a friend of hers told me in old age, there was never any sign of a father, brothers or sisters. She left at fourteen, and by the time of her marriage, aged twenty one, was employed as a machine operator in a zip factory.

My Father's relationship with Ada was not without its difficult moments. On 23rd January, 1942 he hinted at a miscarriage, or abortion: "Had a letter from a friend D lost her little sister, so A. says", though the lack of other reference suggests that he was not directly involved. In September 1944, however, there was a serious pregnancy scare in which he was:

> Tuesday, 15th September, 1944: Had the bad news. In terrible trouble, no rest till I see this right.
> Wed 6th: Very worrying but I have a hunch that I can pull it off.
> Thursday 7th: I got a first start and have given the hint.
> Fri 8th: Still worried looking forward to tomorrow.
> Sat 9th: 2-10 [shift on the docks] Here it is and the works are started what a relief.
> Memo: The worry has been terrible this week
> Tuesday: Succeeded. Must be more careful in future. No more till Xmas Wed: cant say much only very pleased. quiet.
> Thurs 14th: Nearly went mad oinly [?] in time, careful is word.

* * *

Strange to relate, with regard to my Mother, tender emotions were to come into play once again: despite all that had happened, my Father must have retained some dream of a happy relationship with Lily Jones. By mid-June, 1943 he had agreed to another series of assignations. He wrote on the 18th:

> I met my wife at 7.45 at Ravenhill Park. She did not know what to say. Still, at the end of a very long sit-down said she wanted me to take her out. What a hope. I found that my feelings had changed.

When, one Sunday about that time, my Mother instructed me to ask him outright whether he would live with her again, he replied emphatically "No". But in July he was again able to write, uncertainly, "I don't know what to do about her. I know I won't be happy with her."

In the autumn my Mother again started looking for a house. My Father ignored her requests for help – on the contrary, he applied to the court for a reduction in the maintenance payments on the grounds that he was supporting an elderly Mother. He was unsuccessful, and when my Mother found out the meetings stopped again.

> If we continue living as we are, I know who will be most lonely in the end. It wont be me because I have Mervyn he wont always be a boy, he'll soon grow into a man.

She envisaged me as a long-term companion into her old age.

* * *

Things were not made any easier for my Mother by her awareness of the relative ease and opulence enjoyed by her younger sister Annie up in Treboeth. The girls had, I believed, always been rivals, but at first my Mother's matriculation and office job had raised her several pegs. Auntie Annie left school at 14 and was only a tailoress. When my Auntie got married to my Uncle Glyn they also started off in a tiny house, much like our own, in unprestigious Lisbon Terrace.

But things changed and Auntie Annie floated into one of the biggest success stories known in our little world. Uncle Glyn was a likeable, good-mannered man who worked for Mr. James the Coal Merchant, and by dint of honest effort rose to the exalted position of Sales Manager, with a home telephone and a car. He played the violin, and led his own dance band. While we were living in Lamb Street he moved his family into a roomy property in Treboeth with such glories as a third bedroom, a porch, a bath and a girl called Sadie who came to clean twice a week.

Uncle Glyn had a dinner suit and took Auntie Annie to mysterious 'functions' at the Masonic Hall, the barest mention of which made my Mother pale with envy. He did high-quality decorating (unlike my Father) and although he drank, he knew when to stop. His daughter, my cousin Audrey, went to art school, and her brother Donald attended (albeit ineffectually) the private Bible College in Gower. On top of all that, Uncle Glyn managed to suppress his Swansea accent, and overlaid his native Welsh with a hint of Oxford.

As time passed my poor Mother fell further and further behind her sister. The bombing of our house in Lamb Street, the dispersal of our furniture, the need to move in with a crippled mother, the failure of her marriage, and finally the need to 'thump a comptometer' put her at a hopeless disadvantage. Auntie Annie came down to the Hafod once a week, on a Wednesday afternoon, when my Mother was usually in the office, to clean the parlour where Gran slept.

My Mother was not averse to having a confrontation with Auntie Annie, and a good opportunity arose when she once happened to be home during a weekly visit. It was the only polite row I ever heard her in. The four of us were in the kitchen having tea – Gran, the two sisters and myself. Auntie Annie said something like:

"Oh, dear, I done a lot today. I feels quite tired."

My Mother could not let a remark like that pass.

"It's only your duty call. You done a bit in the parlour, that's all. Look what I got to do every day..."

"I got a home and two children to look after as well."

"You got Sadie to come in and clean for you..."

"We've still keeping your furniture from Lamb Street for you, it takes up a lot of room. Glyn was saying only yesterday..."

"Well, I haven't got anywhere to put it, have I?"...

On and on it went, with references to girlhood incidents and old scores that I had hardly ever heard of. Gran sat helplessly in silence. I liked Auntie Annie, and I thought my Mother was being vindictive, so I did my best to stop the row, firstly by turning the wireless on very loud, and then by singing 'God Save the King' at the top of my voice. But it didn't help, for my Auntie was just as unstoppable as my Mother.

Thank Gawd my Mother's not usually at home on a Wednesday, I thought, as Auntie Annie finally put her coat on. "If she was, we'd get this every week."

★ ★ ★

Over in St. Thomas life was getting harder, too. "Starting this year with a very heavy load around my neck," my Father wrote on the 1st January, 1944. "Cannot someone break theirs is my fervent wish." His pocket book, which he kept going for most of that year, again filled with notes about his unchanging routine. Any improvement in the coal trade was unthinkable while the war was on, but he still dreamed of a return to the bounty of the late thirties. He did some work loading sand, but he hurt his back and had to give it up. He found increasing difficulty in meeting the maintenance payments, and at one point fell badly into arrears. "How long this will go on I dont know," he wrote in February, "but it is driving me crazy." "Today is Mervyn and Emrys's birthday," he noted on the 26th July, (it was supposed to be the 25th, actually). "Broke, could not give my boy only best wishes." By a strange coincidence I shared a birthday with his brother, who like my Uncle Jack was at that time still serving in North Africa.

His chest became more troublesome as coal dust and tobacco smoke took their toll of lung tissue. Gamma was getting frailer, too. "I am very worried about my Mother," he noted. "She isn't well at all. But she is really marvellous for her age. And the place and everything else is the same as I remember years ago. I don't know what I shall do if anything happens to her." And a few days later: "Thank God my Mother seems to be OK. again. I had a rough time while she was ill."

Despite these problems, however, my Father doggedly tried to maintain his image as a fun-loving coal-trimmer. Most of his evenings, as ever, were devoted to the Labour Club, the 'Cyprus' (or some other pub) and the pictures. Ada continued to make herself available. "Had a good night again, mutual agreement. Also received a bit of tobacco from the same friend... Looking forward to tonight when I know I will see my old pal who wont see me short... In Jersey Park for a change."

My Sunday visits were still awaited with pleasure and evoked approving comment. "Making a boat, very nice too," wrote my Father. "The questions he asks are extraordinary. A lovely boy."

Oddly enough, this was when my relations with my Father were at their closest. After tea at Osterley Street he and I would sometimes go up for a walk on Kilvey Hill. It was greener on this, the seaward side – no lead fumes, I expect – and quite pleasant to stroll over. We would look out over the rows of houses, including No. 17, the ships in Swansea docks, and the Bristol Channel beyond.

On these occasions my Father liked to talk about his life – or carefully selected aspects of it. He told me a good deal about the First World War – how he had been in the trenches, had gone 'over the top', and been wounded. Some of his mates had eaten soap to make themselves sick and get out of the front line. One had his palm gnawed by a rat while he was asleep, and my Father had seen a horse blown up and transfixed on a telegraph pole. No wonder, I thought, he was a hero when he returned home. Then he might go on to talk about his work – or lack of it, coal for the ship's bunkers or main holds, getting 'stuff' off the dock, how wonderful Gamma was, with the occasional, invariably negative, comment about 'her' (my Mother). Emotional matters concerning Ada and Doreen remained, of course, deep and unrevealed secrets. To me, he was always kind and attentive. He liked being with a twelve to fourteen-year old boy – while lacking any understanding of my needs, emotional or cultural.

Indeed, as my school work proceeded and my horizons broadened, my admiration for his war record came to be tempered by wonderment at his ignorance. There was hardly anything he could talk about outside his own personal experience. If he made a rare historical reference he might be centuries out: and if corrected, he was not in the least perturbed. He did not follow politics (apart from voting Labour) and mocked religious belief. He had no interest in music (except pub songs), languages, or any of the sciences.

Apart from that, we never seemed to get around to the matters that really troubled me: my failure in sport, my fears of bullying, the problems in Aberdyberthi Street. He had evidently been an athletic and pugnacious sort of person; how I longed to hear him say something like: "Come over tomorrow, I'm not working, I'll teach you some boxing" or "Sport? Ball games? I'll see what I can do!" I knew he had no money, but he did have free time. Yet, despite these blank spaces I retained my respect for him. He was, after all, my Father, and in those days the word meant something.

Our walks usually ended at the bus stop near the bottom Danygraig Road, where we took the No. 76. The bus was convenient for me and passed the Labour Club in Wind Street. Getting on it, though, was often embarrassing, for if it was too crowded to take us, my Father would nimbly jump the queue just as the vehicle was moving off, and yank me on to the platform behind him.

"Jump on, son!"

Then, as likely as not, he would try and ingratiate himself with the conductor by giving him the equivalent of our fare while refusing to take tickets. My Mother would never tolerate dishonest behaviour like that.

* * *

The sadness which surrounded me led me to cocoon myself in a world of boyish handicrafts, mainly model ship-building. Perhaps it followed naturally from my involvement in house repairs and my love of sea stories. There was rarely money to buy the tools I needed – a plane, a gouge, a tenon saw: usually I had to wait an eternity before getting them as Christmas or birthday presents. But I persevered.

I began by fashioning a square-rigged man-of-war, making the hull from a rough block of wood, and the masts and spars from slivers of firewood. The vessel had a flat bottom, and although it immediately turned turtle when I tried to float it in our zinc bath, it was well suited for games on the kitchen table. The deck was equipped with miniature lead cannons which I founded myself in a clay mould, using bits of lead piping which I melted down. Indeed, I soon came to regard myself as something of an expert in this field, to the extent that one day my cousin Donny Thomas came down to ask me to help him.

"I'm trying to make some lead planes," he said. "I've got a little spitfire as a model, see. Can you come up to our house and help?"

I was surprised to hear that Donny had tried to do anything like that – I knew he wasn't much interested in hand-work. I agreed.

"What have you done then?" I asked. "Have you made a mould?"

"A mould?" said Donny, "What's that?"

When we got to Auntie Enid's a few minutes later, there was no mould, as I suspected, but Auntie Enid, trying to be helpful, had a saucepan of moulten lead simmering on the kitchen fire.

"Take it off," I cried, "It'll tip! Donny, you've got to make a mould first."

"'Ave 'e?" said Enid.

My memory of what happened after is dim, but I'm sure Donny got no further... Back in No. 64 my man-of-war was followed by an elaborate schooner, with capstans, hatches, running rigging and features which would, I think, have placed her in the mid-nineteenth century. Unfortunately, her keel kept breaking off, so by the time she was completed, her draft was too shallow, and she capsized as well. She ended up as a wreck in the garden shed. Over in Osterley Street my Father caught my enthusiasm, and refurbished an old fin-keeled yacht for me. He painted her red and blue, and Gamma stitched a set of sails. It was my Father's supreme effort at shipbuilding. One blustery afternoon I carried her up to Hafod park, where there was a large open water tank. Alas, no sooner had I set her on the rippled surface than she turned turtle like the man-of-war and the schooner. So another dream faded.

My only really successful effort at shipbuilding was the schooner called the *John L. Jones*, which I mentioned in my diary. Graceful, well finished, painted blue and white (though without canvas), she was placed on the sewing machine cover in the kitchen. Boyhood dreams can be long in fulfilment: I had to wait a decade or more for my first real sail under canvas, and that took place not in Swansea Bay, but in the distant waters of Massachusetts, long after my Swansea boyhood had ended.

My Mother was also trying to take her mind off things, though with the help of (a) religion and (b) politics. An obvious place of refuge, on Sundays at least, was Mount Pleasant – our family had always been Baptist. There was no Baptist chapel in the Hafod, so sometimes, after tea, my Mother would don her best outfit, make me dress tidily, and take me down to the service.

Mount Pleasant is, as one can see to this day, a somewhat imposing building. When we arrived the pews would be almost full, for the minister, a Mr. Pollock, was very popular. He wore a dog-collar and a strange black cassock with an extra fold of material over the shoulders, like a nineteenth century overcoat. My Mother enjoyed his sermons ("they're very positive, and they makes you feel nice," she would say). Mount Pleasant was a musically-orientated establishment, with a built-in organ and a large bannistered area for the choir. Sometimes one of the regular worshippers, a well-built girl in her mid-twenties, would be invited into the pulpit to render a devotional song. When she got going her great breasts would heave with effort, but my Mother did not appreciate her performances. "She looks down on people," she would whisper, "too snobbish for my taste." In the course of the service a group of deacons, among them no less a figure than Mr. Cox, who taught English at Dynevor, would come around with large collection trays. Usually you could see how much the people next to you had given.

The great moment in the Baptist year is, of course, the baptismal service, and on one such Sunday my Mother took me to see it. We went up to the balcony to get the best view. An extraordinary number of children, otherwise never to be seen in chapel, were there already. When I looked down I found that the floor of the choir area had been taken up to reveal a tiled basin filled with water. Mr. Pollock gave his sermon, and after it was over descended, *fully-clothed*, into the water, which came up to his waist. Then the coy supplicants appeared, dressed (it would seem) in their pyjamas, and Mr. Pollock lowered each and every one of them backwards for a moment until he or she was completely immersed. Every time a body went under, the choir (now re-located to the front pews) would strike up a loud refrain:

Ha-lle-lu-jah, Hallelujah, Hallelujah,
Ha-lle-lu-jah, Hallelujah, Hallelujah,

Hallelujah, Hallelujah,
Hallelujah to our King

which in Swansea was pronounced Halleliew-ya. I thought it was wonderful. After their brief ordeal the newly baptised were wrapped in towels and rushed off to get dressed, before they caught cold.

My Mother's woes, alas, outlasted Mr. Pollock, for after a year or two, the deacons decided on a change of minister. As he was sitting in the pulpit, waiting to give his last peroration, Mr. Pollock broke down in tears. People looked at one another in embarrassment, though I found it riveting. "Did you hear about Pollock?" Florry Luxton asked us, a few weeks later (she was 'big' at Mount Pleasant and knew everything). "He went to a chapel in Bristol and had a nervous breakdown. Now he's in a mental hospital."

His replacement, a Mr. Emrys Davies, was from the valleys and a very different kettle of fish. He used to break into song in the middle of his own sermons, singing little snippets like "Happy day, oh Happy day, when Jesus washed my sins away". Unfortunately, he was a bit too forthright for my Mother. "He's always on about sins and going to hell" she told me. "I don't like it". So she discontinued her devotions.

She had always voted Labour, and some time after we moved to the Hafod she decided to join the Party and became a good Labour woman. "Good Labour woman," Gran would say in disgust, thinking of her darker sides. But she was no doubt glad to see my Mother go off to ward meetings of an evening, so that she could enjoy peace and quiet at home.

"I want you to come to the ward meeting tonight," my Mother said on one occasion. "It's only up the Hafod School. Percy Morris, our M.P., is coming to give a talk on his trip to America."

When we got there I found a room full of middle-aged women, with nobody of my age at all. My Mother was anxious for me to sit towards the front, so that Mr. Morris could see me. He turned out to be a small, engaging man with glasses. He had come to entertain, rather than inform, so he picked out topics which he thought would be of interest to his constituents. In the US, he related, he had been invited to functions for which, he was told, he required a tuxedo: not only did he not have one, but he did not even know what it was. He regaled us with the story of how he tried to find out without revealing his ignorance. It was, we learnt, a dinner jacket. Then there were the American breakfasts.

"They only gave us one rasher of bacon," he said, "but there were two eggs, both fresh. You could have them scrambled, boiled or fried, and if they weren't turned over, the Americans called it 'sunny side up'."

In Britain eggs were rationed, and eating two was regarded as a virtual impossibility. People who didn't keep chickens as often as not had to manage with egg powder. (In fact, in the end I got to like the powder more than the real thing.) After the speech, my Mother took jolly good care to push me forward into Mr. Morris's benign gaze.

"This is my son Mervyn," she declared. "He's at Dynevor!"

Mr. Morris beamed at me for a moment, like a good constituency M.P., before turning to someone else. He was the most famous man I had ever met.

* * *

Quite unexpectedly, in the summer of 1946 my Mother had a new reason for contacting my Father. As I had duly noted in my diary, I started to go lame on my left leg. Doctor Harrington up Green-hill said it would certainly have to be investigated further. My Mother wrote to my father withn the results on the 15th June, 1946:

Dear Billie,
The presumptive diagnosis was 'fibrositis', which I understand is a muscular complaint. I sincerely hope for Mervyn's sake that it is nothing very serious.

I dont know how you feel about things now Billie, we have been apart for such a long time. Of one thing I feel convinced and that is that you are not happy. I dont excuse myself for everything – we should have lived happily together for Mervyn's sake. But I have this consolation and I shall have it to the end of my days, that I did everything that it was humanly possible for a woman to do to try and get you back to me and Mervyn. I have always treasured the pleasant memories our married life and cast out of my thoughts the unpleasant ones.

I shall let you know all there is to know about the result of Mervyn's X-rays and I sincerely hope there is nothing seriously wrong with him.
        Yours,
          Lil.

Her hope, however, was not to be fulfilled. On 30 July she wrote:

I suppose you know by now that our boy went into Hill House Hospital last Friday. He is allowed to write a letter home on Monday's and I am enclosing a copy of what I received from him today. Visiting is very restricted because Hill House is really an Isolation Hospital and although Ward 5 where Mervyn is, is the Orthopaedic Ward they have the same restrictions imposed. Only half an hour from 3 to 3.30 on Sunday is allowed and then I only see him through a glass window. I am sure his little heart is as heavy as lead.

Write to him Billie and encourage him. Will you? Don't depress him with anything of our past. Help him to feel that he has you as well as me to look to and to lean on. He is only a child and very sensitive and tender hearted.

All I know is this, that if I can't get to feel different he wont have me to come home to.

Yours,
Lil.

P.S. Mervyn was top of the Form.

Dear Billie, only one visiting card is issued which admits both parents and if you want to come along with me on Sunday or any other day please let me know, then I wont take anyone else with me. I get there by 2.30 in order to be there so that I have the longest possible time with Mervyn.

Yours, Lil.

My Father did indeed write to me, but never took advantage of her offer.

Six

Hospital Days

It was clear to me, as my Mother and I trailed past the damp rhodo-dendron beds in the hospital grounds, that another big change was taking place in my life: Lamb Street, Aberdyberthi Street, Gwen-draeth, and now Hill House. Hill House was basically a fever, or 'isolation' hospital, and the single-storied wards were scattered over a green hillside. One of them, however, was used for children's orthopaedic cases. We found a long, low building with an entrance and ward office in the middle. Behind, as I soon discovered, was a veranda with a lovely view over the gorse-filled valley to Cefn Coed, the mental hospital where my Auntie Beatrice so often found solace.

We were met by Staff Nurse Taylor, a small bespectacled woman with a strange resemblance to Tojo, the maths master at Dynevor. She was a business-like creature, for whom I was just a routine admission. To my utter dismay I heard her tell my Mother that she could take my clothes home, as they would not be needed. Visitors, she added, could come during the weekly visiting hour on Sundays and see me through the ward window: they were not normally allowed inside for fear of infection.

My Mother went off in tears, and Nurse Taylor led me down the immeasurably long ward, with small children, all boys, on each side. I found it strange because I had never been in a hospital before. When we got to an empty bed, she gave me a horrible white nightdress thing, which had to be put on, or so it seemed to me, back to front. I looked at it with distaste.

"Put this on, will you?" she said. "The tapes tie up at the back. How long you'll be here? Months, I expect. When you're undressed I want you to have a bath."

A few minutes later she took me to a cavernous bathroom with an enormous fixed bath. By now I had sunk deep into an awkward, resentful mood. Too many bad things had happened too quickly.

"I'm not getting into that awful thing!" I said. At home we had a homely zinc bath which hung on a nail out the back; I used it once a week, my Mother less frequently. Poor Gran could not get into it at all.

"What?" said Nurse Taylor, amazed. "You won't bath? I'll have to call Doctor Alves. She'll tell you."

I was only persuaded to change my mind when a stern Scottish woman in a white coat appeared, and threatened not to treat me if I persisted. Thus began my stay in Hill House. Things got worse, much worse, as the afternoon drew on.

"You haven't been eating enough vitamins, fresh fruit and vegetables," said Nurse Taylor testily, as though it were my fault. "Not enough calcium! That's why your hip bone is soft."

She was dead right about the fruit and vegetables – my Mother always skimped on fruit, and (as I have noted) we only ate salad on hot summer days.

"You'll be getting Vitamin C tablets and malt every day, now," she went on. "Here's your first dose."

The malt turned out to be a sickening brown gooey substance which had to be swallowed by the spoonful. The main part of my treatment, though, was to be much more drastic.

"We've got to take the weight off your femur, so that it can grow again," said Nurse Taylor. "You'll be going on a frame."

This, she explained, was a leather and metal contraption designed to keep me pinned down horizontally, so that my femur could be pulled slightly away from its socket. But as the frame would take some time to construct, I would start by having my bed put on 'elevator blocks'. They were brought a few minutes later – large bulbous pieces of wood about 18 inches high which were placed under the foot of the bedstead, so as to make it slope backwards.

"Get on to it, will you?"

In no time at all two other nurses appeared with long strips of sticking plaster which they attached to my legs. There were tapes at the ankle ends and these were tied to the bedstead. I subsided on the hard mattress.

"It'll take a week or so for your frame to come through," said Nurse Taylor as she looked down on me. "Try not to lift yourself up on your elbows, it won't do you any good." Then the nurses all went off, leaving me sloping, head downwards, in a totally unfamiliar world.

The whole procedure had been so sudden, unexpected, and unfriendly! When suppertime came I found that I did not like the food, apart from the fact that eating and drinking with my head lower than my feet was no easy matter; let alone the two other things, with horrible bottles and bedpans.

Oh, my Gawd, I thought, how can I stand this?

* * *

I decided that my hospital experiences, like my life in the Hafod, should be recorded for the perusal of a grateful posterity. So on the second or third dreadful day I got hold of pencil and paper, and started an occasional diary. I also filled my letters home (post was accepted once a week only, as it had to be fumigated) with detailed accounts of what I observed around me. My Mother, with loving care, kept nearly all of these missives.

* * *

The main event of the week, as I quickly discovered, was the visiting hour, when the parents would come hurrying down the drive and cluster around the ward windows, shouting to make themselves heard through the glass. On the first Sunday my Mother brought my Uncle Jack and Florry Luxton. Jack tried to be cheerful, while Florry peered at me through her glasses, and assured me that when someone was in hospital it was much worse for the relatives, who were left worrying at home. How the hell, I thought, can that be worse than lying in a bed head down? I didn't say anything, though. My first letter was written just after that visit. I was initially under the impression that I was in Ill House, reflecting the condition of the occupants.

Ill House, Ward 5
(Posted 30th July, 1946)

Dear Ma and all,
I am sorry to tell you but the nurse says I will almost certainly be here for 12 months. It was after all a waste journey to bring me my jigsaw and droughts. They are more strict with me now and I cannot even rise to my elbow, so I can only read.

I do not suppose I will be able to hear you at all next Sunday because the window was open a little last Sunday and I was able to raise up on my elbow. Next time the window will be shut and I shall have to lie down flat. It will be worse again when I go on my frame.

I have not had those things yet that you brought because they have to be fumigated. I ate some breakfast this morning.

Some of the boys are walking about this morning and it makes me envious.

Fondest Love from Mervyn
P.S. Please write to me. M M

A week later, after my Mother's second visit, I was trying to pull myself together a bit:

> August 5th
> Dear Ma,
> After you had gone home I remembered more things I wanted so now the full list is:
> 1. My small French Dictionary
> 2. My Diary (and the other things I told you, books etc.)
> 3. My Jack Knife
> 4. String
> 5. Please go to Woolworths and by me two yards of two colours, making four yards. I want the plastic FLAT stuff, to make bangles like the last one I made. Please buy bright colours. I do not want the plastic tubing.

At this point Matron, a small, trim and obviously strict lady, made her first appearance in my letters. She wore a dark blue uniform, like the ward sisters, but was distinguished by a white wimple-like head-dress. You couldn't miss it.

> Dear Ma,
> A moment ago matron came along. The first thing she said to me was, "Who told you that you would be here twelve months?" I said "Miss Thurston, the orthopedic nurse." She said, "Miss Thurston has nothing to do with it. It all rests with Dr. Pew [Pugh] and Dr. Parker. You may only be here three months and it mostly rests on yourself. Eat well and keep your "sprits" up".
> Well, that is what she said condensed down into a few lines. You see, she held a very optimistic view of things, so I don't want you to worry or vex, as I can assure you I will do neither.
> Please write often and tell me all about the niebours. It is suppertime now so I must close with
> Fondest Love from Mervyn to his Darling Little Ma and to Jack and Gran.

Despite the optimistic tone of this letter, and my attempts to busy myself, I found the first few weeks in Ward 5 hard to bear. My ankles were still attached to the bedframe a foot and a half higher than my head, and much of the hospital food was uneatable. But at last, on the 22nd August, there came relief: my 'frame' arrived. When the porters carried it in, I gazed at it in wonderment. It was a Y-shaped contraption of metal and padded leather: my legs fitted into iron stretchers at the V angle, and there were breast bars designed to keep me prostrate. It looked like an instrument of torture used by the Spanish Inquisition.

I was lifted on to it straight away, without being permitted to sit up, and the breast bars were bent over. The sticking plaster and tapes on my legs were retained, so that my lower limbs could be pulled away from the pelvis; groin straps held me in position.

In fact I was absolutely delighted to get on it. Although I could no longer rise to my elbows, and my head would be a few inches further from the window on visiting days, I was at least back to the horizontal. As for the further outlook, I was told that a few months on the frame would be followed by a long period with my legs in plaster, when I would be able to sit up. Finally, when the femur fully recovered, I would be encouraged to exercise until I was strong enough to walk. It was, however, going to be a long process.

* * *

By now I was quite familiar with most, if not all the faces in my new, confined world. Although all of the children on our side of the building were boys, most were too young to share my interests. The only person of my own age was poor Stanley Towell, a lad who had a crippling disease of the legs, and knew he would never walk properly. He had been in hospital for years and though we were on friendly terms we had little in common.

The staff, I soon realised, were grouped into distinct layers, one above the other. At the bottom of this admirable pyramid were the probationer nurses (like timid Nurse John); above them there were three or four grades, up to the senior nurses (Taylor, and Nicholas). The colour of their uniforms varied from pea-green to dark blue. Most of them were rather motherly and caring, but there was one, Nurse Evans, who went a little further – sometimes a lewd glimmer would appear in her eye, and once she suggested that the loin cloth I used when being washed should be replaced by a bunch of parsley. She had a tendency to grab me, and say things like "There's lovely he is, isn't he?" rubbing her starched apron against my face. I didn't like it, and decided that she should be treated with caution.

I had not been in the ward long before I realised that I had a problem with the nurse-in-charge, Nurse Nicholas, a big, fat woman with thick glasses. She would march down the ward with a peculiar, sweeping gait, as though carrying all before her. Her cap was always set low over her forehead, possibly to indicate the need for discipline. She was also an enthusiastic chapel-goer, and occasionally hummed hymns while going about her ward business. However that may be, we took an instant dislike to one another, and I promptly termed her 'the walking mountain' which came out as 'la montaigne qui se promène' in French. Somehow, perhaps through reading my letters before fumigation, she found out about it: and relations deteriorated further.

Above the nurses, and below Matron, were the ward sisters and sister Tutor, another tall, imposing lady who taught the nurses how to nurse. The specialist orthopaedic nurses, Misses Thurston and Tuck, had their own clinic in town, but came in to inspect us every week. They were dressed in white coats, and I was somehow struck by their serviceable, flat-heeled shoes. The team of doctors, Tigh, Pugh, and Alves, was headed by the all-powerful orthopaedic surgeon, Mr. Parker, though he worked in distant Cardiff, and made only occasional visits. Finally came Jack the porter and a couple of unassuming women cleaners who would get things for you from other parts of the ward if you asked them nicely.

★ ★ ★

School work was organised in the ward, and I found that the lessons (together with the homework) took up a large part of my time. The teacher was Miss Evans, a glamorous thirty-year-old who appeared daily, dressed in a white coat like the doctors. She admitted to me that she was not very good at algebra, for her talents did not lie in that direction. On Monday, 2nd September, 1946, I wrote

> Dear Ma,
> School started today, and Miss Evans, our teacher, went up to Waun Wen to get some books, and Miss Matthews asked about me, so Miss Evans expects great things from me in art... She asked me to help her teach some of the younger pupils to read, at least those who can come to my bed.

At the same time more advanced teaching had been arranged for me through Dynevor – Mr. Cox, the English master, was to come up and tutor me twice a week. My relations with him were excellent, and although I still found much of the work boring, there was at least no P.T. or bullying.

> Mr. Cox came this morning [I wrote a little later] and stayed an hour and a half with me. He said he managed to palm a lesson off on a student teacher, so he could stay that much longer. He said

some terrible words to me, 'Blinking and Devil'. I nearly looked at him in surprise. He must be taking after me. He spells my name Myrddin, and starts his letters Dear Myrdd. He is not a bad sort really. I was thinking, if I had taken up Latin I would have been good at it by now, with Mr. Cox a Latin master as well...

There was also a scout group, well served by Mr. and Mrs. Adams – whom we were told to call 'Skip' (Skipper) and 'Arkela'. They were a diminutive, friendly, pair, one fat (Skip) and one thin (Arkela). Skip, I learned, worked as a labourer in a scrap-yard down the Strand, close to the place where I bought tar. I marvelled at his strong, thick fingers. The pair were devoted to the scouting movement, and gave up their Saturday afternoons to come and see us.

Despite all the ward constraints, and my horizontal posture, my hobbies had to be pursued. So I asked my Mother to bring in parts of my Meccano set which I could assemble when lying down, together with bits of wire to make an electric magnet.

This last day or so, I have made a sort of passenger coach to run along a cord from the opposite bed to mine. It acts very well and we get lots of fun. I think there is some very thin copper wire in the shed with no insulating tape on it. Its diameter is only about the size of this dot . and there is about at least 60 ft of it. If you can find it please bring it for me...

Many other small events were duly recorded.

I passed my Tenderfoot in Scouts today, and I am well on my way to 2nd Class. Stan and I are learning Morse code like anything.

(My Father had, of course, been a signaller in the Infantry.)

Our beds were taken out on the veranda today, because it was fine. I don't like it much. I had to make a map for the schoolmaster, of the district of Hafod, etc, and it blew onto the boiler-house steps. I had taken about three days on that map, and I only just managed to get one of the boilermen to get it back for me ... I think I have a lot of freckles on my usually handsome contenance but I am not sure. Anyway you see me so you know.

I clean my teeth now as often as possible but I have no means of telling whether they are clean or not. Lately I have had an idea. The chromium on the sides of my watch provides a good mirror although very small.

Today I had a letter from Dad, and he said he was going on some outing with the coaltrimmers or something if Gamma was better. I think it was to last several days, because he was also going on several char-à-banc trips, to Cheddar, Bristol, and Coventry. Yet in the same letter he says he has to stay in with Gamma as she is bad. I think it fitter for him to try and see me, although I do not miss him in the least.

And some reassuring thoughts for the folks at home:

> I hope Gran is alright, please give her my fondest love, and tell her I think of her often. I hope there are not so many rows at home because they have a bad effect on everybody concerned.
> Thank Aunties Annie and Edith and also Uncle Glyn and Jack for coming to see me.

> Je suis très heureux. Ma forme est très confortable, et je ne suis pas en piene.

My daily reports, however, were soon to lead to a second clash with the authorities (that is, following my unwilling induction in the ward). Since our letters had to be fumigated, they were handed in unsealed. The senior nurses in the Ward must have regularly read much of what I wrote – and had misgivings about it. I reported on Sunday 29th September:

> I have not been able to write since Thursday as the Assistant Matron says I did not ought to write in diary form. Nurse Taylor said that she reported it to matron. She says it impedes my education.
> I have written very small this time because I dont want my letters to be too thick. By the way, I think I would like a telescope for Xmas.

* * *

The hospital food was an increasing problem: fortified by my Mother's midweek pasties and weekend pies, I was eating ever less of the dreadful stuff. It also assumed a prominent place in my letters.

> After school finished in the morning I gathered together my courage and braced myself for the ordeal of dinner. I ate (I shouldn't say 'ate') I masticated it all (as is my custom) and had a read to calm myself down afterwards. We had cups and saucers instead of mugs last night, it was indeed an occasion...
> I don't think you have better let me have that chicken on Sunday, if Nurse won't take it. I would rather you eat it yourself than have it in illegally as it is so difficult to eat it without anyone knowing. You have to be so catious that that fact alone spoils the pleasure...

I ate more than half my dinner today but if I waste much my name will go down in a book for Dr. Tigh to see. You must not bring me up any pasties in the middle of the week now, partly because I am getting a bit tired of them but mostly because Matron is tightening up the regulations. I will see if you can still bring up pies.

In addition, something funny was going on in the ward kitchen:

Today when I opened my box of things which is kept in the kitchen, I saw that a little piece of my Crunchie was missing. I told Nurse Lake who was in charge and she said that if the person who took it is not found she will tell matron. I marked it off into little divisions, one of which I ate every day. That is why I know. It is not the Crunchy I mind it is the principle of the thing.

My reluctance to consume the common fare (like everybody else in the hospital) could not but come to the notice of Matron, who decided to take things firmly in hand. I wrote on the 13th of October

It was just dinner time and they were putting the dinners out, Matron came down to the ward and went into the kitchen and put my dinner out herself. Then she put it in front of me and watched me eat it.

When I had nearly finished she scraped all the gravy together and tried to make me eat it. I said, 'It would make me sick. I don't like the gravy.' Her fury was aweful. She did not say so much but you could see it in her eyes.

She said, "You couldn't have been used to a good dinner at home". I said, "I always had a good dinner at home, matron". Among other remarks she said, "Good food make you sick indeed," and "I wish I'd known about this before." Dr. Pugh came to see the baby Roger, and she told the tale to him. When she came out of the Ward office she made a last parting shot, "I'll be here again tomorrow", or the equivalent. You could tell she was really angry.

By the way, you had better not bring a pasty in this week because I am not very popular with matron at present. I really mean it.

★ ★ ★

I knew little about developments at home, and my Mother never referred to them directly in her letters: but I tried to monitor the situation as best I could from the snippets of news, mostly bad, that filtered through.

Jack told me last Sunday that you and Gran are always arguing. I don't like to hear that and I will ask him every week how you are getting on. Don't forget what I have said.

It is very foolish of Jack to keep on going around without a hat because he has already caught about seven colds and he will catch seventy more if he keeps on with it. But I know that whatever anyone says to him will have no effect because he wont listen. What has become of that bike that Jack bought, is it still up Treboeth? Tell me in your next letter.

I managed to get Jack's birthday card posted. I tried to get one of the nurses to get him some hair oil but she wouldn't and another took the money but returned it.

I received your letter this morning and was surprised to read of Auntie Hannah's death. There are certainly a lot of things happening at home in my absence. By the way, I always thought the name was spelt 'Anna' and not 'Hannah'. Anyway, it is too late for that to matter now.

I hope Gran is O.K. I have not mentioned her in my letter for a long time but I think of her very often. I hope her legs are not too bad.

I viewed most of the children in the ward with a somewhat jaded eye, and commented on them frequently.

All the girls have been moved over the boys side because they are spring cleaning the girls ward. When they have finished that ward they will take us all over the girls ward till they clean this one. At present all the girls are over here and beleive me it is simply aweful... We'll be glad when all this shifting is over and we are back in our own Ward again without those girls.

Peggy Thomas was terrible in school, she used to shout "Miss Evans is a fool, She makes faggots on a stool", etc, in front of Miss Evan's face. After complaining about four times to matron Miss Evans has got her shifted over the girls ward.

That Ivor Howard went home today and I was never more glad to see anyone go. He wasn't all there and he was next to me and he used to babble from morning to night.

Some of the kids have got dyarea and they have been put over the girls' side. I think the pong must be terrible. When the visitors will be coming on Sunday they will be saying "Where's my John?" "Where's my Edwin?"

Edwin is going home on Monday. He has been here about a year, I believe and has been on a frame all the time. He is a very funny little boy, and can tell fibs by the yard. If someone said he did something he repeats "No I never" all the time. He can nearly walk by himself, too.

Most people think that Alan is incurable. He might be going to the Prince of Wales hospital to try and be cured there. I think some new patients are coming in. One has an amputation.

A boy of about nine years came in today but he is only a tonsilefony. That means that he had his tonsils out but they started to bleed. He is also called a bleeder, and he has to have a sort of tweezers in his mouth to grip his tonsils and stop them bleeding.

I very unwittingly made Stan cry today, simply by saying he was a slow writer. Of course, I said I was sorry a dozen times, for I had no idea how much I had hurt him. However, we palled up a bit after that. He will be going home soon, and the next oldest boy, Terry Evans, will be home inside a month. When they go I will go skatty with only kids around me.

* * *

In the middle of October, however, I got wind of a possible change in the social situation. In one of my letters home I made a first reference to the person who was destined, through his very presence, to bring it about. Of course, I could not vouchsafe for the accuracy of the rumour which reached me.

There was a doctor's son in Morriston Hospital (I wrote on the 13th of October) and from what I heard from Miss Thurston he was rather – I can't think of a suitable adjective, but anyway he has broken the bars of his frame, etc., etc., and is very sure of himself and thinks himself very clever. He was in a cubicle in Morriston Hospital and he was a private patient there. The nurse who had to fetch him in an ambulance said his mother was allowed to stay with him all day and read to him.

He has some sort of paralysis I think that is catching for he has to stay in a cubicle [in Hill House] for six weeks. When that period is over he will be coming down this ward. I am looking forward to his arrival in spite of his ways. He will be company for me at any rate.

* * *

Late one evening, shortly after I wrote those lines, I had an unusual, indeed unique, visit. Most of the lights were off, the younger children were asleep, and the day staff had long since left. The ward was at its quietest, and I think I was reading. Suddenly, the shadowy double doors at the end of the ward opened, and in walked no less a personage than Dr. Pugh. He made straight for my bed, drew up a chair and sat down. His deliberate manner suggested that he had come on a serious mission.

"I'm told," he began ominously, "that you've been in a certain amount of trouble."

My mind raced round in circles. Which amount was he thinking of? I had done my best to keep most of it under wraps, allowing only passing mention of it in my letters home. I thought the best thing to do in the circumstances was to sound him out, one incident at a time.

Was it perhaps the on-going feud with Nurse Nicholas, after she found out that I was calling her a Walking Mountain in French? My complaint that she would only let us listen to sermons on the wireless on Sundays? Being cheeky to Miss Evans? The bother I had had with Nurse Smith, when she had cut my nails too short?...

Dr. Pugh just sat there in an anticipatory silence.

Breaking the school leather-punch on a piece of tin? Saying "You again?" to Nurse Andy? Making a Meccano leg scratcher to reach my itchy calves, thereby loosening my sticking plaster? Upsetting probationer Nurse John after she read about her Uncle's death in the Evening Post (by asking whether he left her anything)? Annoying Skip by losing some of the scouting books in my locker? Or was it not eating the hospital food, the illegal pies, and Matron?

Although, in the end, I fully unloaded my conscience, Dr. Pugh still made no clear response, only asking me a few general questions about school. "Do you get much homework? Are you keeping up with your lessons? Etc., etc.... Well, good night, then!" He left as suddenly as he had come, giving me absolutely no idea of the reason for his visit. I switched the light out, a very puzzled boy.

The incident was swept from my mind one morning early in November when Michael, the doctor's son from Morriston, made his triumphal entry, borne on a stretcher by two ambulance men. Tall, thin, and immediately likable, he wore an expensive dressing gown, spoke with an Oxford accent, and exuded all the subtleties of a superior culture. Anyone less like the unassuming Stan Towell it would be difficult to imagine. One of the first things he told me was that he did not drink tea for breakfast. "Can you order coffee in this place?" he asked. I was flabbergasted – surely everyone in Britain had tea for breakfast?

"I caught polio on our family trip to Switzerland," he explained airily. (He meant poliomyelitis, which I had never heard of; it was a disease which apparently destroyed muscle.) "I got it swimming in a lake. There had been no problem when we went to France and Austria, you know."

Though he was strongly built, Michael thought the disease might leave him with a slight tremble for some time. He had a metal and leather frame as well, but it was much more elegant than mine, without the spread-eagled legs. And he was allowed off it to do exercises daily.

He professed a negligent attitude towards school work, and delighted in finding easy dodges. "Never do today," he told me, "what you can get someone else to do tomorrow." He knew about roulette and gambling, and (unlike me) had started Latin. He disdained the boys' weeklies which I read, and in so far as he read a newspaper at all, it was *The Times*. "Did you know they make grammatical errors in it?" he said. "I read an article about it." I was flabbergasted again. He had a miniature camera, and before the polio caused muscular problems had been enthusiastic about photography – something much too expensive for me ever to consider.

His father dropped in to see him shortly after he arrived – as a doctor he had unimpeded access to the ward. He was a quiet, unassuming Irishman, and not only a doctor, but a consulting pathologist as well. (I didn't know what 'pathologist' meant either, but I was doubly impressed: in fact he dissected corpses.) Michael also revealed that there were bishops on his father's side of the family. Though not actually rich, they were obviously well-to-do. I first saw his Mother when she came to the ward windows, like everyone else, the following Sunday. Well-dressed and charming, she was from Pembroke, and spoke a deliberately refined English. I could see, peering through the glass, that her mere proximity threw my Mother into a spin.

After so many months of childish company I was overjoyed to have someone like Michael close by. The reason for Dr. Pugh's visit now became clear: he had come to check my suitability as a daily companion. What with all the trouble I had been in, I wondered how suitable I was...

7th of November
Dear Ma,
Life is much more pleasant since Michael has come for there is someone of your own age to talk to. I hope you are not worrying about me because I am perfectly all right, in the best of spirit, health and happiness. I hope you are in the best of everything like I am too.

Then I continued in school-boy French:

Tonight Michael et moi nous avons été écrire des poèms de

Nourice Nicholas, et Michael a dit Nourice Nicholas d'eux. Il a dit Nourice Nicholas de ses poèm et elle ne l'amait pas. J'ai pense que irais à Ward 4 aujourd'hui parce que j'étais un méchant garçon à la Nourice de nuit. Le père de Michael viens le voir toutes les nuits.

[Tonight Michael and I have been writing some poems about Nurse Nicholas, but Michael told Nurse Nicholas about his, and she did not like it at all. They may be sending me up to Ward 4 [a sort of recognised punishment] because I was cheeky to the night nurse. By the way, Michael's father comes to see him every evening.]

...Except from the ordinary worries which schoolboys have (school, etc), I am quite happy here in this ward. Michael and I would like a pack of cards to play with but I don't know whether they would be allowed. Anyhow, if you have an old pack at home could I have them please? If matron did object she would only tell me to send them home, and that could be easily done. Of course, don't send a pack of cards in if it is the only pack you have....

Michael had some games in today including Monopoly, Snap, Belisha Militere, Speed and one or two more. We planned to have a nice game of monopoly tonight but nurse would not move our beds together and we could not play. I received your parcel today, though why you should send me two a week is beyond my comprehention. (I hope I spelt that correctly).

* * *

In the middle of December an opportunity arose for me to get out of the hospital – at least for a few hours – as I had to have an X-ray in another part of Swansea. I guessed my Mother would be interested, so I wrote to tell her about it.

We will also be having our X Rays shortly, though I can't think why you want to know. You won't be there to see me (well I hope not anyway), and when they are carrying me from the ambulance I will put a blanket over my head not for the passers by to see me for I would be very self conscious (I don't think I spelt that right either). I wouldn't feel to sure of myself on a stretcher. Anyway the ambulance ride ought to be O.K.

The visit to the X-ray centre, however, turned out to be more stressful than I anticipated. The centre was located in one of the large houses in Walters Road, and my huge Y-shaped frame, with me strapped on it, had to be carried some distance along the street. The blanket did not help much, and passers-by looked on in astonishment. Sure enough, on the pavement outside the house, stood my Mother, bathed in tears. That was the worst part of it. Why had she come? She couldn't speak to me. But in the letter I wrote on returning to Hill House I expressed no anger.

I felt very sad when I saw you crying today. You shouldn't have waited all that time for me to come out of the X-ray place, it won't do your feet any good. Miss Thurston told Michael that I was the best Perthé in the ward, and that I was very lucky. As you said your-self, Michael's father would rather Michael have what I have than the paralisys. Tonight is one of the saddest nights I have ever spent.

★ ★ ★

Meanwhile I continued to record life's little ups and downs, as before.

Mr. Cox said that he would be coming during the [Xmas] holidays, but he was laughing and his face belied his words. I dont know how much truth there is in the matter, but I am not working during the holidays. I am also up to my neck in work this week. The Scout master has given us a dollup of work as well for he won't be here again for a fortnight.

I received your letter this morning in which you said you hoped that the Scarlet Fever had cleared from the ward. I think that the danger is pretty well over now. I also think that you have been worry-ing far too much about the Scarlet fever. You forget that I am in the place for Scarlet Fever. We get our temperature taken after tea and about five o'clock in the morning and the place is alive with doctors.

I am on the sixth chapter of *Great Expectations* so far and I think it is an excellent story. I am contemplating asking you to stop the *Rover* and *Adventure* and just continue with the *Wizard* and *Hotspur*. Perhaps in stead I will get the *Everybody's* because I find them very interesting and educational.

The light was cut here last night and we were in the dark for about twenty minutes. I made a thing out of my meccano to hold a battery and bulb so I had some light. That is the second time that that has happened. When the lights fail, the nurses have to carry oil lamps about. They are pretty dim and cast a very weird glow. There is a boy in this ward called James Davies. Well he is very jittery and is in the last bed. When the lights go out we cannot see him and we tell him so and he begins to weep and cry because he is afraid that "a man with a black bag will come and get him."

The barber came this week and when he left I was almost bald. However, I suppose it is better that way. I have just received Jack's letter and was delighted to find it was written in French.

Then, on the 19th of December, there was more important news.

Tomorrow Mr. Parker will come from Cardiff and I am looking forward to his coming eagerly. Tonight is a night of suspence. It is a curious fact that since I have been here I sleep pretty lightly and wake up on average about three times a night for water. I am in a daze, have a drink and go back to sleep.

Mr. Parker brought good tidings indeed.

I AM COMING OFF MY FRAME [I wrote immediately after his visit]. I will be coming off after Xmas when Miss Thurston and company limited come back from their holidays. We were waiting for Dr. Parker to come and all of us were highly strung up. Then he came to my bed and said, as he looked at my Xray, "this looks terribley good." Then he said that I would have to go into plaster, and I will be able to sit up. So I want you to be happy over the Xmas and not mope. Michael has just come off his frame too. Stan will be going home soon too.

Meanwhile, preparations for Christmas were proceeding apace.

The twelve days of Xmas start tomorrow, [I wrote, not very accurately, on the 21st of December] with school finishing, the School party, scout party, cinema show, Xmas Day, Boxing Day, and the puppet show. It will be as good as one long party.

We will probably be going over the girl's ward for the School party today, Ex patients will be coming in so we (Michael and I) have suggested to Miss Evans (she will be coming) that all those that are up should play 'Kiss in the Ring' and 'Postmans Knock'.

I forgot to describe the tree. It holds two dozen fairey lights, and Matron sent down some Chinese lanterns. Then there are some tit bits like aeroplanes, silver rings, lucky horseshoes, etc and there is a fairy doll on top. Father Xmas (in other words Sister) gives us gifts from the nurses on Xmas Day. We get our presents from home on Xmas morning. I think I will enjoy this Xmas after all because I had such a good Xmas present off Mr. Parker. I had a terrible birthday present because I came here on the twenty sixth of July.

In the event Christmas Day started rather early.

The time is Xmas Morning, twenty to six. I have opened all my parcels, and I have had piles of stuff. I had a smashing propelling pencil from John Halfs with which I am writing this letter. I had a parcel from Milky [Bryn Clifford] and I had a parcel from John Lewis...

But the most valuable and the best present was my telescope. The sight of it took my breath away. It is a real beauty. I almost feel like scolding you, it must have cost pounds and I know you can't afford a lot. I must stop writing now because I have a lot to do, such as eating sweets, spying, going through my books etc.

And later in the day:

I hope you didn't worry about me eating my dinner today, because I am telling the truth when I say that I enjoyed it. We had sprouts, turkey or goose, roast potatoes, boiled potatoes and apple stuff. I had Xmas pudding after dinner but I don't think it was nice. I will see about mine.

Finishing the same letter at the end of the week, I added:

Sometimes I get Sister to open the window and then I can spy through my telescope. I can see a road with some houses and a common in front, and every detail clearly even to the wireless ariel and the letter box. I can even see the leaden pattern on the window.

I hope you all had a very Merry Xmas and Gran enjoyed herself and had "a drop of something" to her taste. I hope Jack enjoyed his first Xmas at home, and that he will never have to spend any more of his Xmases abroad. And above all, I hope my dear mother enjoyed her Xmas.

★ ★ ★

Yet, on the fringe of my family circle, Christmas had been darkened by tragedy. A copy of the *Evening Post* for the 23rd December, which my Mother sent me a few days later, carried a report of it on the front page, next to an unnerving article on the shortage of poultry ("...Only one regular customer in ten will be lucky to return home with the old-time familiar sight of a turkey's legs sticking out of a heavily laden shopping basket...")

FAMILY IN BLAZING HOUSE

Three members of a family living at Lisbon Terrace, Treboeth, Swansea, jumped from the window of a bedroom when their home was ablaze early today.

One of them, Mrs. Edith Hannah Matthews, wife of the occupier, was later taken to Swansea Hospital with leg injuries. Her husband, Mr. Richard Hubert Matthews, bus conductor, received some bruises, and similar slight injuries were received by their daughter Elizabeth Harriet Matthews.

They were aroused about 3.50 a.m., when Mr. Matthews found that a fire had got a good hold of the downstairs middle room.

An alarm was raised, and National Fire Service men were quickly in attendance under Divisional Officer George Hay. They found flames coming through the front door, but soon got the blaze under control.

The fire having spread to the staircase, the family above had no alternative but to get away through the bedroom window, which was about 12 feet above ground level.

The family went to bed about midnight, and it was the presence of smoke in the bedroom that gave the first indication to Mr. Matthews that all was not well. Considerable damage was done to the house and furniture.

I could not fail to record my pained reactions, for we were on good terms with Auntie Edith and Betty, having been down to Gower with then not long before. The Lisbon Terrace Matthews's were in fact a different Matthews, but related to us through Uncle Glyn's marriage to Auntie Annie. Auntie Edith, one of my Mother's few friends, was a slim, active woman who once did a lively kick dance in our kitchen, stretching out her left arm, shoulder height, kicking it with her left foot, crying "Oh, Chrisht!" the while. On reading the report I wrote to my Mother:

I was very sorry to hear that Auntie Edith's house was burnt down. I am eagerly awaiting more news. If her spine is injured she will probably have to have her neck and back in plaster so that she will not be able to sit up at all. Uncle Hubert and Betty must be in a sorry plight, for they have nowhere to go and no property. I suppose they will be years getting another home together, that is, if they can.

It was a pity Auntie Edith lost her head and jumped out of the window, because if she had not panicked she would have escaped with little or no injury. But I suppose she was half asleep. They might even have made a rope of blankets and lowered themselves to the ground. But there is no good in saying what they might have done because it is all done and passed now. I was sorry to read in your letter that Auntie Edith fainted when all the people came to see her. Sorry for all those smudges, but the nurse just spilt some water over my letter.

* * *

One of the least noteworthy events of that time was my Father's first visit, which took place just after the Christmas holiday. He had never taken up my Mother's invitation to share a Sunday visitors' card, presumably to avoid the embarrassment of meeting her. I had no forewarning of his intention, – he must have persuaded Matron that he could not manage to come at the regular time.

Suddenly, one weekday morning, a nurse rushed up to me. "Your Father's coming down to the Ward," she said. "I'll pull your bed around the window." Michael heard her, and I could see him straining from his bed so as to keep the hospital path in view. Knowing him as I did, I was surprised that he exhibited such curiosity.

A few minutes later my Father appeared in his usual jaunty attire, his thin face wreathed in a smile. I can't say that I was particularly moved when I saw him: despite his letters I knew that his concern for me was much less than my Mother's. Anyway, we tended to write only about tools or things I needed for my handicrafts.

"Hello, son," he shouted through the glass. "How are you? Gamma sends her love!" We tried to talk for a few minutes longer, but there was a lot of noise inside the ward, and little to be said anyway. Finally he gesticulated towards the ward office, suggesting that he had left something there, grinned, said good-bye, and went off. I reported to Mother

Dear Ma,
Dad came to see me yesterday. He brought me two small books, ten bob, and a box of chocolates. Five of the ten bob was from an Auntie. The wireless was going full blast and I did not hear all he said.

★ ★ ★

The year 1947 began with the momentous change decreed by Mr. Parker. I was as delighted to get off the frame as I had been to get on it: sitting up was wonderful. Two plaster casts, which could not be removed, held my legs in the same V position with a crossbar just above my ankles. But now I could slither around the bed (in fact they gave me two, because I needed a second to support my ankles) while Miss Thurston encouraged me to exercise my upper parts. I soon learned to stand on my shoulders, hoisting the plasters in the air. The Sunday visits were easier, too, because I could get right up to the window pane and hear the visitors better.

The winter of 1946-1947 was one of the coldest in living memory, but our parents continued to appear behind the glass, frozen to the bone but smiling.

It is awful to be able to look on the snow and not be able to go out in it [I commented in January]. I don't suppose it will snow again now for about five years when I am about. By what I hear things seem terrible outside. All these old electricity cuts, no coal, snow, no food, must make life hardly worth liveing. It had to come at the most awkward time, too, just the critical point of the governments plans. I read in the paper last night that the cause of it all is an anticyclone centred over Norway and Sweden and apparently this is diverting the winds from northern Russia over here. All I can say is that I pity the people in Northern Russia.

One morning, inside the ward, the nurses tried to involve us in snowy games.

We have been having a bit of fun with the snow today, I wrote. Everybody has been throwing it at everybody else. I moved over to the window, opened it, and I got some snow off the windowsill. Everybody who could walk or stagger was outside playing snowballs. There was plenty of snow on the windowsill so I was able to join in the fun to a certain extent. Then Miss Thurston, Tuck, Evans and some nurses took a tray outside and began to tobogan on it. I got a lump of snow and threw it at a nurse who got more snow and tried to stuff it down my neck. I called Miss Evans to help me but she helped nurse instead. I got Miss Evans lovely later though.

Unfortunately, the school term was looming again.

I don't know what it is but there doesn't seem to be any time to do anything. I wake up between six and seven, breakfast lasts till eight, and then I do my exercise till school starts. I get about three quarters of an hour spare at dinner time and about two and a quarter hours spare in the evening. I don't know where the time goes to.

Michael misses about an hours school every morning because he has to do his exercises etc.... I wouldn't like to be him when he has to go back to school, but there, I think he is going to start at Clifton [Public School in Bristol]. I'm glad I'm not going there.

And in a lighter vein:

You know that Miss Evans put some tadpoles in a large goldfish jar on the table. Well as soon as they got big they just used to disappear, presumed eaten by the others. Well today some one had a bright idea and at the time of writing they are swimming peacefully about in an old bedpan. I don't know what our honourable teacher will say when she finds out.

By the way, have you any chickens left now? Tell me in your next letter.

School did, however, prompt some unexpected stirrings on the literary front. The fact I liked keeping a diary, and had tried to do one or two short stories, never led me to think that I could write much. But one day, to my surprise, Mr. Cox raised the matter.

Mr. Cox sent me a copy of our school mag. and suggested that I wrote an article for one. He may have been joking, anyway, I hope he was because I could not write an article...

I decided to have a go, nevertheless.

I have finished that story for the School magazine. I have always fancied myself as an author and Mr. Cox urged me on by saying I have style. The jobs I may go in for now are as follows: Engineer, Draftman, French Master, and Author. I am considering going in for law, but I don't think that job would really suit me. The story that I have written would be much better if I had planned the plot in more detail.

Please excuse the rambling style of this letter but I haven't much to talk about as you know and I've just got to write about what comes into my mind first.

★ ★ ★

Now that I could sit up it seemed natural to extend my handicraft activities, and they waxed ever larger in my diurnal round.

I want to tell what I want this week: a pair of pliers, a small light hammer and a small file. Then I would like a tube of strong glue because it often comes in handy.

It was not long, however, before my noisier enthusiasms came to the attention of Matron.

I was knocking nails in the top of the [telescope case] I am making, and making a devil of a row when in walked matron and saw me at it. She didn't say anything, though. However, when Miss Evans came in on Monday morning she came straight to me, and said in her Bright Idea voice, "I've got an idea". The school Inspector will be coming soon, and she thinks that he ought to find us doing something. So she offered a prize of a poetry book to the one who would make the best topical scrap book. (Newspaper cuttings etc.) Well as I don't get newspapers I suggested that I make a book of pressed flowers and leaves and that is what I am making now.

Michael for his part encouraged me to take an interest in photography, though I didn't have a proper camera. Again I hoped my Father would help.

> I asked Dad about sending that old camera in if it was any good,
> but he said that he had taken it to a camera expert [I suppose it was
> some old coal trimmer like himself] and he had said it was no good,
> and was a job for the firm who made it. I put a rather nasty piece
> about it in my letter to him. I said, "If the camera <u>expert</u> has seen
> that camera and said it is no good I realise that there is no need to
> send it in. I will ask my mother to see if anything could be done
> with that old box camera at home." That's what I said, tell me if you
> think I did wrong.

The usual grudging response ensued:

> I had a letter from Dad in which he said nothing about the folding
> camera, but he said that that box camera in the Hafod was his. Well
> he's had it, or rather I had it and I'm going to keep it. I hope you
> will bring it in today.

The old box camera duly arrived with some film to practice on.
In addition, Skip and Arkela got Michael and me to start learning
First Aid, and model trains came into it as well:

> Michael has had his [model engine] controller in and we have tried
> his engine on a piece of track. It goes quite well but it doesn't start
> quick enough. A tiny piece of metal called a "brush" fell out of it
> and it doesn't go now, so Michael has told his father and he is going
> to send it back to the makers.
>   I realise your good intentions, but I hope you don't bring my
> *Caerphilly Castle* up for Michael to see, because it is really a poor
> model and he has three Hornby engines of his own.

There was also a distinct improvement on the food front.

> Since I have been getting adult food (late suppers etc.) and espe-
> cially during these last two months our food has improved
> imensely. For supper we get, soup most of which is extremely
> tastey, kippers, mackrel, poached egg on toast, cold meat (occai-
> sionally, not often with pickeled cabbage). That's all I can name
> offhand but we can always have sauce or vinagar if we want it with
> of course, pepper and salt.

But now I was beginning to have a weight problem:

> I have decided that I am getting too fat, so I am going to try and

cut down to five half rounds of bread and butter a meal instead of six or seven. I will gradually decrease until I reach three or four pieces because I must not be too heavy on you when I get home.

* * *

Meanwhile, my letters continued to provide comment on various other matters as viewed from my bed in ward 5.

Milky wrote to say that Dynevor has been connected up with a school in Rennes France and that the boys were to write letters to one another. I don't know whether I will get a pen pal, I should love one, but I hardly like to ask because I am in hospital. I can't do anything so I suppose no one would want to write to me.

Have they collected the gasmasks yet? If not please try and hang on to mine because I would like to keep it as a souvenir.

I received your letter today, and read of the Whist Drive that is being held to help Auntie Edith out of her difficulties. I wish I could help in some way. I am going to write her a letter now, but it is going to be a difficult task as I will have to be very tackful.

I am going to write to Auntie Kate to thank her for the money she has been sending me every week. She is very kind. I have had at least forty shillings off her since I have been here.

Just before you came last Sunday some boys came to the big common of gorse behind the hospital and set it alight. I managed to open the window and I saw the lot through my telescope. Some boys were passing by, and next minute there was a big blaze. I don't know exactly whether they did it, but I wouldn't bet that they didn't.

Nurse Taylor has just told us that Stan Towell has had an accident. He apparently has broken some bone or other in his leg. He went out in the snow. He is at present at Swansea Gen. Hospital, but he may come up here. It seems as though the hospitals do not want to let him out of their cluches.

Another thing I forgot to tell you. We had a little sweep just before the Derby. Miss Thurston thought of it, so just as he was announcing the race we all drew, at 3d a ticket. I drew Pearl Diver and won about four bob. Not bad.

* * *

Despite my absorption in school work, hobbies and exercises, my problems with the higher authorities were by no means over. One day, at the end of January I aimed a wet prune stone at a boy called Billie Stukie in the next bed. Although the stone missed him he complained vociferously and the matter went right up the chain of command to Sister Tutor. She made it her business to come down to the ward and tell me off ("not the sort of thing a grammar school boy should do"). Mr. Cox, supportive as ever, just laughed it off. "What a lot of fuss about one lousey prune stone," I wrote.

It was, however, to be the prune stone which broke the camel's back. One morning soon afterwards two of the hospital porters came in and pushed my two beds to the far corner of the ward, a form, I thought, of banishment from centre-stage. I was livid, but could do nothing about it, at least in the short term. True, Michael was now partially mobile and could get down to my bedside: but what would his parents think? And my own family? I suspected that Nurse Nicholas was behind it. A fourteen-year old who tried to lead an active life and disliked sermons was more than she could take. However, Jack's suggestion, after a Sunday visit, that I was in disgrace, provoked an outburst of righteous indignation.

> I was very surprized Sunday when Jack said that I was down here through bad conduct. If he thinks so would he kindly ask nurse about me? I have been making inqueres as to if I could be moved [back] because I don't like it much here. I find that it has something to do with matron. I think my two beds look untidy in the middle of the ward... I will try every blinking chance I have to get shifted back.

My relative isolation, combined with my ever more adventurous exercise programme, soon led to my most serious transgression ever. One evening early in April, when I was standing on my shoulders, with my plaster-encased legs in the air, I overbalanced and fell out of bed, though fortunately without hurt or injury. Perhaps I could have heaved myself back up, had I so desired: or perhaps not, because the plasters were heavy. But since I was actually on the floor, and there was no nurse in sight, I decided to slide around and do a little exploring.

In any case after a few minutes of glimpsing hitherto unseen localities, including the mysterious service room, I called the duty nurse, who, seeing me on the floor, promptly panicked. ("Oh, my God, what has he done now?") She called another nurse and the two of them somehow lifted me back. I was lucky that Nurse Nicholas was not there, or she would certainly have vested some dreadful punishment upon me forthwith. Night descended and I thought that was the end of the matter: but it was not. Next day I had a flurry of important visitors.

There has been a terrible commotion here. I fell out of bed yesterday evening but fortunately I did not hurt myself. The nurse was a few minutes coming so I made my great mistake. The service room was only about four yards from me and I have always wanted to see inside it. I pulled myself over to it and thence to the table.

The assistant matron and the matron are not very pleased about it, to say the least of it, and neither is that Dr. Alves. The Staff Nurse in charge, la montagne qui se promène, Nurse Nicholas, added a few things against me, such as that she has had to shout at me when doing my exercises. That made them think that I do not do my exercises properly, but I do.

I was standing on my shoulders when it happened, but thank God I am all right. I am tired to death of all the fuss...

And a little later that day:

Matron came around again today and she seemed deadly calm. She firmly believed that I was mucking around when it happened. The assistant Matron firmly believed I had fallen out of bed twice. They threatened to tell Dr. Tighe about me.

You seemed very peturbed about me falling out of bed and of all things breaking my back [I continued a few days later]. I've never heard of such a soft thing in my life. It is like as if I am sitting on the edge of a blinking precepice. I don't like falling out of bed and falling out of bed is a very rare occurance. I don't suppose I will fall out of bed for another three years. Besides, when I do my exercise there is always a nurse by me now.

My Father made his second visit shortly after this had happened.

Dad came to see me yesterday. He came about half past eleven. He brought me some sweets but I couldn't have them because for some reason the nurses wouldn't take them. I haven't seen him for so long that don't know whether he looked bad or well.

He never came again: there were just the two visits, though my Mother clocked up about fifty.

* * *

Much more spectacular was a visitation from Michael's extraordinary aunts. "They're missionaries and they work in Persia," he had once told me, in a most matter-of-fact voice. "They're headmistresses or teachers or something. I think they met the Shah."

The Shah of Persia, I thought. Jesus!

One Sunday during the visiting hour I suddenly found two swarthy womens' faces peering at me through the glass. They were, however, beaming.

"We're Michael's aunts from Persia," one of them said, "I'm Auntie Nooee and this is Auntie Emily. We're home on leave."

"Oh, thank you for coming," I said.

"We hope you'll be well soon," said Aunt Emily.

"Gawd bless you," said Aunt Nooee, who seemed to be a little older.

I was completely overawed. They spoke with soft Irish accents and said 'Gawd', like most people in the Hafod, rather than 'God'. My Mother had retreated from the window in her usual confusion. How lucky Michael is to have aunties like that, I thought, not my lot, like Auntie Annie and Auntie Olive and Auntie Beatrice. They had a present for him, too...

They brought him a smashing little electric motor and it goes nice. It is very tiny, too small to work anything, but I am going to try to make one tomorrow or bust in the attempt. (I am nearly busting as it is). I would be glad if Jack could get me a book on dynamos from the libarary, just one that explains all the principals and different types. I find that First Aid book very useful and I have put a brown paper cover on it. Michael has had a map of Pembroke made in 1620 or thereabout from his Father.

★ ★ ★

The next important event which to relate was, alas, of quite a different order. It was front-page news in the *South Wales Evening Post*, on the 24th April 1947.

MUMBLES LIFEBOAT CREW SACRIFICE THEIR LIVES
40 Seamen Perish in Gale
Empty life-boat found upset beside the wrecked ship

Probably the worst sea disaster in the stormy history of the South Wales coast occurred last night when gale-lashed waves dashed the 7,000-ton steamer 'Samtampa' on to the rocks of treacherous Sker Bay near Porthcawl, with the loss of 40 men.

To add to the tragic weight of the blow was the loss of the crew of eight of Mumbles life-boat, which was swamped and overturned on her second mercy-mission to save the hapless crew of the breaking vessel.

The life-boat men perished alongside the doomed 'Samtampa', which had split into three parts, after being flung on the rocks and pounded by the huge seas.

Returning after failing to make contact with the steamer on her first trip, the life-boat went out a second time shortly before eight o'clock. No news of her was received during the night but early this morning a report by radio was received by the Swansea police that the upturned life-boat, with no sign of any members of the crew, had been found washed up in the region of Sker Point.

On the sand dunes early today lay four bodies recovered from the seashore, completely black through being soaked in oil.

Mr. H. J. Kluge, secretary of the life-boat, today told a reporter: "It is a terrible tragedy. All the crew were Mumbles men."

The gale-whipped seas foiled an attempt by the steamer's crew to launch one of their life-boats, and the men withdrew in the stricken vessel. That was the last the the life-saving people saw of them.

Then as darkness fell, bodies were washed ashore – lit by the light from many car headlamps focused on the steamer. A reporter who went out on foot with the police and rescue squads when the tide had receded waded up to his knees in oil.

When the life-boat left the slipway she had to go with the gale from westward which was estimated at 70 miles an hour. There was visibility of about five miles and the life-boat could be seen from the Pier having a difficult time.

I have just heard of the terrible Lifeboat disaster at Porthcawl [I wrote after reading the article]. I was horrified when I read it in the *Evening Post*. Forty seven men killed and only a few miles away. It must have been dreadful for the people on the shore to watch the ship being dashed to pieces before their eyes, and not be able to do anything. I wish I was up and active, and did not have to stay here, But it is all for my own good and it won't be long now.

I also had a letter from Dad, but he didn't say much in it, only that it was terrible on the dock when the Lifeboat got wrecked and that I would have to learn more in morse.

★ ★ ★

The Lifeboat disaster was, however, soon swept from my mind by a happening of far greater importance (to me personally that is, not in the annals of the town). It found no place in my letters because it was much too intimate. One night I had an exciting dream about just catching a ship before it sailed. It was a paddle steamer with reciprocating machinery. I experienced a strong pumping motion in the engine room, and woke to find myself embarrassingly wet. Yes, the time had come for me to enter the male portal. It was what I had heard about so often in school.

Fortunately all the patients were asleep, and the night nurse was in her office at the other end of the ward, so I could clean up unobserved. Being in a far corner had its advantages, after all. The sensation was a bit scary to begin with, yet there was no doubt in my mind that it was definitely the most exciting thing that had happened to me at Hill House – far better than Xmas, or even release from my frame. I couldn't tell anyone about it, though, least of all Michael. I sensed that he was far too reserved about such things.

★ ★ ★

At last, on Thursday, 15th May 1947 I came out of plaster.

> I had a bath and I remember it was nine months today that I went on my frame and ten months tomorrow I came here. I mean lunar months. My legs are tender and I can only bend my knees about three inches but they will come. Mr. Parker said that I am to get up in a month, or five weeks. You can fetch my pyjama trousers in now. I am on a single bed. It seems very narrow after being on two beds for so long.

Then Mr. Parker himself came down from Olympus – or at least his hospital in Cardiff.

> The great man came today. He turned my knees in and pushed my legs far apart. Then he caught hold off my big toes and started to shove my legs around with them. Mr. Parker thought that my movements were very good. He seemed in a terrible mood, but I think that is natural.
>
> Miss Thurston told me to ask you for boots in, but I am not sure whether she meant boots or shoes. You must phone up just to make sure.

And two weeks later I stood up. I wrote on Sunday, 1st June

> Big news. much to my surprize, I got up last Thursday and stayed up. I could not stand up straight and I felt as though the floor was one great magnet drawing me down. My shoes arrived after dinner so I put them on and Miss Thurston tried me walking along the veranda rail. She thought that I walked very well. I had tea in my pyjamas at the table in the middle of the ward with Michael. Michael gets on a sort of wheel chair and although he is not really supposed to, he pushes himself along.
>
> On Friday I lost that pulling feeling and today I can take about two tiny steps by myself. I am very grateful to God for what he has done for me.

150

Michael and I knew that we would be leaving the hospital about the same time, and we both looked forward to it greatly. But in the event his parents came to collect him rather unexpectedly one day after lunch. There was a lot of fuss and bustle as his Father helped him to get his things together, and the nurses carried them out to the car. I stood in the driveway and watched in silence.

There was little to be said: he knew my address, and had promised to contact me. But as I watched the old family car drive off, I felt unutterably sad. And although it was ridiculous for a boy of my age, I shed a tear. After so many months of Michael's company, I experienced a strange feeling of emptiness. His parents had, I knew, taken a house in a posh part of Morriston, while I was very much a Hafod dweller. Apart from that, his going to Clifton meant that he would not be staying in Swansea for long. The circumstances of any meetings would be different.

Consolation, however, was not hard to find – in a day or two I would be leaving Hill House myself. I appreciated the care and attention the hospital had bestowed on me, yet I had no emotional attachment to it. I had got on reasonably well with the staff (except, of course, Nurse Nicholas and occasionally Matron), but I was not really close to any of them. My going would not be missed: patients were passing in and out all the time. So as soon as Michael's car had disappeared I made my way unsteadily back inside, and started packing myself. Before too long a hospital ambulance would be taking me back to Aberdyberthi Street.

On the evening of Tuesday the 1st July, 1947 I penned my final words on life in Hill House.

> Tonight, God willing, will be my last night in hospital. As I lay here, in my hospital bed, my thoughts drift back along the channels of time, to the days when I first came here. I can see clearly, in that "inward eye which is the bliss of solitude" [note the influence of Mr. Richards, Hafod School] myself walking down the ward with a slight limp, and with a somewhat greater temper. I did not know what was in front of me and I was afraid. A few weeks later I started my life of crime. I have never been in anything serous, though, thank God.
>
> I have been suffering from eye-strain of late, and as the light is failing I had better close my reminiscences until I am calm enough and have sufficient time to continue them.

SEVEN

PASSAGE OF TIME

My first impression, on staggering into the kitchen at No. 64, was how tiny the room had become. It was all very inviting, with my Mother in an unusually relaxed mood and Gran smiling in the corner; but living in a large hall for a year had profoundly changed my perception of space. I got used to the house again in a few hours, not least because everything else was unchanged. The same could be said, alas, of the tensions which had pervaded it. Relations between my Mother and Gran, bad before, seemed to have worsened considerably. Moreover, Gran seemed to have had a small stroke – in any case she had started to squint. Her paralysis and incontinence were worse, and in the days and weeks that followed there were moments beyond description, though the memory of them was to remain with me for ever. It still did not enter anyone's mind to have her medically examined.

I could not understand why my Mother was so impatient towards her. It might, I thought, be her way of expressing her frustration at life, the absence of a husband, the need to go out working every day (though she valued her independence, too). In any case she would start bickering with Gran before she went to work, and resume when she came home. I would always wake to the sound of them quarrelling downstairs. My Mother, though intensely concerned about my own welfare, seemed to lack any element of pity for Gran, regarding her only as an extra burden. Auntie Enid came in to help, as before without receiving a penny for it. As time passed Gran got really frightened of my Mother. "Oh, help me clean up a bit" she would cry when I came home from school, "She'll be home soon". And to my Mother: "Leave me alone, can't you see, I'm only an old cripple!" I loved Gran more than anyone, and kissed her forehead when she wept. "The only peace I'll ever have," she would say, "is when I get to Cwmgelli". That is where the family grave was.

Perhaps not surprisingly, my return from Hill House was soon followed by a profound change in my attitude towards my Mother. The last elements of childish love, evident in my letters, were increasingly banished by the negative qualities that lurked in her. I don't know whether it was simply a consequence of my growing up, or a fuller recognition of her ill treatment of her own Mother. But apart from that I was dismayed by her nasty comments about other people, her temper, her easily-provoked hysterics. Her ineptitude about the house became ever more irritating. I knew she was still working hard for me and loved me: but I began to feel that she was the fount of much unhappiness. And although I wished her no physical ill, I came to long for her disappearance, – just like that – so that Gran and I could live together in quiet amity.

Things were eased, thank heavens, by the presence of my Uncle Jack. He was spending his last few weeks at home before going off to a teachers' college in Bangor. Though he was only ten years older than I, serving in the Air Force and travelling abroad had matured him greatly. Somehow he knew how to stop my Mother's quarrelling and bring an element of calm into the situation.

"For Gawd's sake, shut up, will you?" he would yell. And for some reason my Mother would do so.

* * *

It was only now that I got to know him really well. He was physically quite unlike me being short, stocky, fair-haired, jolly – and beer-loving. Again, unlike me, he had a wonderful way with people and masses of friends. He was trying to be creative, and was writing a memoir entitled 'A Dog's Life' on a battered portable typewriter which he had bought cheap. Most of the work, as far as I could see, comprised an account of a long hitch-hike he had done through Europe after demob. It was never published, but to his credit it was the only book ever written at No. 64, and doubtless in the whole of Aberdyberthi Street. Apart from this authorial endeavour, his four years in Egypt made him something of a hero in my eyes (rather like my father in my earlier years), and I greatly envied his plan eventually to study in France.

Jack still showed great respect for my schooling, and encouraged me, as before. But he was not very clever, and though no genius myself, I felt it whenever we talked about anything serious. He would, for instance, tell me long jokes which were hardly funny when he got to the end, and hardly justified the narrative. One day I told him that edible plastic ducks had gone on sale in Swansea market, and for a moment he was inclined to believe me.

He could be a bit tiresome about the house, as I had found when he first returned home. He had a hard time in Aberdyberthi Street, what with my Mother, Gran, no proper washing facilities, and (worst of all) a double bed shared with me. Miss Thurston had insisted on a hard surface when I got home, so my Mother had turned the iron frame upside down, and laid the feather mattress on the cross-bars.

"Jesus!" said Jack, when he first laid down on it, "it's like a rack for medieval torture."

In fact it was much less comfortable than my frame at Hill House, so after I had been home a few days I started sleeping on the floor again, as I had when Jack returned from Egypt. The frame was turned springs-up again so that Jack could recline in comfort.

After a few weeks, I found I could get about more easily, and considered doing a few much-needed household repairs. I decided to ask Jack to help me tar the coal house. It had formerly been Gran's Anderson air raid shelter, but had been dug up and positioned next to the house. As a consequence of my long absence it was going rusty. He agreed, though a little reluctantly. So one fine morning, when I knew he would be in, I went down the Strand, bought half a gallon of tar, and brought it back, balanced on the handlebars of my bike. When I carried it in the smell pervaded the back yard. "I got the tar from down the Strand, Jack," I said, as I handed him one of the dumpy tar brushes. "With two of us, it shouldn't take more than half an hour!"

"O.K., boy," he said.

I set to on the corrugated metal, leaving Jack to get on with the easy bit – the wooden door which I had made from orange boxes. After a few minutes I clambered down to see how he was getting on. Disappointment awaited me. He had no idea how to do it.

"Gawd, Jack," I said. "You can't put tar on like that, in tiny dabs, like a bloody French impressionist. It's TAR, not oil paint! We'll be here all day! Do it in long swipes like this!"

I showed him, – but try as I would, I could not get him to do it properly.

"Mervyn," he said in the end. "I'm not very good at this. I'm going out to meet my pal Cyril West. Good job I haven't got any tar on my hands, isn't it." So off he went, and as I had suspected I had to do nearly all of the job myself.

Little did I realise what was behind it all: for some inexplicable reason my Uncle was beginning to take an interest in art. And many years later, long after my boyhood had passed, he was to become a well-known Swansea painter, with work hung in the Glynn Vivian art gallery. He never had any training, and couldn't draw for love nor money; but he was enthusiastic and loved colour. He painted the little houses and chapels which lent so much character to the Hafod and Green Hill. Back in 1947, however, his artistic leanings did not fit the needs of the household, especially where tarring was concerned.

★ ★ ★

The coal house was only a beginning. As soon as I could walk properly I determined to transpose the house into the twentieth century, through two great initiatives. Firstly, there was the need to improve access to the lav at the bottom of the garden. As it was, you had to go down an uneven earthen path, lined by long and usually wet grass. To remedy this I bought a few bags of sand and cement and in the course of two or three days' hard labour laid a long walkway so that you could get there without stumbling or getting your legs soaked. (You still needed a torch or candle at night, though.) It was not a difficult job, but I wore the skin off my fingers by pushing the wet cement into nooks and crannies. I had never done anything so ambitious before, and when it was finished I gazed at it with unbounded admiration. Then I installed a modern lavatory pan and a holder for toilet paper. My Mother made no comment (she was used to the old ways) and Gran was too weak to make the distance, but the work, when completed, made me feel better.

My second initiative involved nothing less than the installation of a sink in the back kitchen, with a water supply from the lead pipe in the yard. That meant that we would not be for ever carrying bowls of water in and out of the house. I bought a second-hand sink, only slightly chipped, from a yard down the Strand (it may have been Kramsky's) and fixed it, complete with draining board, against the inside wall. Then I made a hole in the wall for the water to come in, and another for the drain to go out. I pushed the new copper pipe, with the tap already attached, through the first aperture. That was the easy part. It was a fine Saturday afternoon, just right for a plumbing venture.

All that remained was to close the mains cock under the pavement in the street, warn the neighbours that I was cutting off the water (four houses were involved), make a hole in the lead pipe in the yard, and solder the copper pipe into it. I breached the lead and set to work on the soldering, using a roaring old paraffin blowlamp. Actually, it turned out to be much more difficult than I anticipated, as I had to melt a thick slab of solder and make the joint, without melting the lead pipe itself. My Mother and Gran waited apprehensively in the kitchen. I did the best I could, switched off the lamp, and enjoyed the silence for a moment. It was all done! Then I went out into the street and opened the cock.

Immediately there were screams from inside the house, and I rushed back in, leaving the cock open. My Mother was out in the back yard, wet and bedraggled, while a huge spray of water from the ill-soldered joint soaked everything, including the kitchen window. My plumbing skills had proved hopelessly inadequate for the task.

"Turn it off quick," she shrieked, "the whole bloody place will be flooded. It'll get into the kitchen!"

"What have he done now then?" Gran whined. "There wasn't any need for it!"

I ran back out into the street and closed cock, while one or two neighbours, including, inevitably, Marge Stanbury, looked on with interest. Something had to be done quickly, if only on account of the other houses which were left without water. I returned to our back yard to check the leak. Sal Jones next door stuck her head over the garden wall – she was always sticking her head over the garden wall – to see what was happening.

"I've got to get a plumber straight away," I told her, breathlessly. "Do you know anyone?"

"Well, there's Thomas in Jersey Street," she said. "You can go down and look for him. Mind, he might not be home, yet. (She meant from the pub, of course.) We'll have to have the water on soon, though. Our Jackie's coming home from his shift, and he haves his bath on Saturday."

I hared off to Jersey Street, and to my enormous relief found the plumber, a small, unobtrusive little man, with the usual cloth cap and canvass bag. Sensing good earnings, he agreed to come up straight away. In a few minutes he had 'wiped' the joint, as they said, and checked that it was not 'weeping'. Then he charged us an outrageous ten shillings for the call-out. "Is ten bob all right for a Saturday afternoon?" he asked. My Mother was very angry, but he had to be paid.

As calm re-descended, and the dishes were washed for the first time ever in a kitchen sink, I felt that I had moved the household forward once more. Later came the installation of a second-hand table-topped bath with a gas cauldron to boil the water. That was easy, as the water went through a rubber pipe from the tap, and there was no plumbing.

But I got a man in to connect the gas: I thought it was wiser.

★ ★ ★

One Saturday, soon after I came out of hospital, there was a knock on the door. I was having breakfast in the kitchen, and my Mother was still in her curlers. I think Gran must have been up in Treboeth.

"Who can that be?" my Mother said. "Go and see, will you?" We did not normally have any callers at that hour. I went and opened the front door, and was astonished to find Michael standing outside.

"Oh, it's Michael," I cried. There was a commotion behind me in the kitchen and I knew it was my Mother panicking. Michael had obviously come with the intention of maintaining our friendship. His Mother and Father were sitting in their car at the kerb. Since we had no telephone, they had no way of telling us they would be coming. Michael's Mother opened the car window and smiled at me.

"Come in to the house!" I said, trying to hide my embarrassment.

My Mother, I knew, would be completely overwhelmed, despite the fact that she had met Michael's parents so many times at the hospital. The good lady probably guessed as much, because she waited for a moment or two in the car, to allow the shock wave to pass. Then she majestically entered No. 64, followed by Michael, squeezing her way past the handlebars of my bike in the passage. Her hair, as always, was nicely permed, and the perfume she wore was just perceptible over the smell of fried bacon. My Mother was so embarrassed that she could hardly speak. But I noticed that she had got the milk bottle off the table, and had put a scarf over her curlers. Michael looked a little uneasy, too: I guessed that he had never been in a home as poor as ours before.

"Oh," said Michael's Mother brightly. "Delighted to see you again. How is Mervyn getting on? We very much hope he can come up to Morriston and see Michael from time to time" (she smiled at me again).

"Oh, yes," said my Mother, "that would be very nice."

"If it would be all right, we could drop in tomorrow afternoon and pick him up, and then take the boys somewhere in the car."

It was quickly agreed, and the visitors left, whereupon my Mother lapsed into a kind of stunned silence. Michael's parents had evidently decided that I would be a good companion for him, especially as the polio had left him with an uneven gait (like me).

In any case, I soon found myself invited to their large house in

Morriston, near the hospital where Michael's Father worked. They had a telephone, a bathroom, a fridge and all modern amenities, like Uncle Glyn but their car was much larger than his. Michael's mother had a sister (Michael's third aunt) called Alice who was a school teacher; their Father, she once told me, had bred prize chickens, so she knew all about poultry.

In fact Michael's mother liked talking about all manner of things. "A hen turkey is much nicer than a cock," she once told me. "The flesh is sweeter... My Father would have bred horses if he'd had the money. But he did leave me a certain amount of property which I took into my marriage... I don't care what people say, a woman's marriage makes her life... I've always taken an interest in bridge, it's a very stimulating game... whatever education Michael ends up with (he can be very lazy, you know), I hope he develops consider-able charm." She loved being a medical consultant's wife, and had in fact trained as a pharmacist herself. She always gossiped without malice. At the same time I found, as I got to know her better, that she had a keen concern for social niceties, or the conventions, as she called them. "Michael," she would say imperiously, "observe the conventions!" Fortunately this did not preclude her helping a boy from the Hafod.

Michael's incredible aunts from Persia also appeared in the Morriston house, looking more tanned and mysterious than ever. Anyone more different from Michael's Mother it would be difficult to imagine. Auntie Noo went on talking about 'Gawd' in a deep rolling voice, and spoke reverently of the Shah. Michael was quite irreligious but would not tolerate any jokes about his family's eccle-siastical connections. "Going to church," he once told me loftily, "is a good insurance policy. If there's anything there after you die, you're in line to benefit." The Morriston house had a lawn with lovely apple trees, and on one or two occasions we had tea under the branches. Michael's Mother made marvellous sponges, but the tea was always too weak for me, quite unlike the black brew we had in Aberdyberthi Street.

Michael and I had some very happy hours together, not least assembling his model railway; he needed my help because his hands trembled slightly. But alas, summer was coming to an end and within a few weeks the family would be moving to Bristol so that Michael could take up his day-boy place at Clifton College. I would be starting back at Dynevor, but I imagined we would still keep in touch.

Outside No. 64 the Hafod was changing, and Swansea with it. The war had inhibited change for years, but change was inevitable. It came in dozens of little ways that I noticed bit by bit, as time went by. Good food had always been close to our hearts, and now strange, but tasty items appeared in the shops: Italian and Polish salami, pasta, pickled gherkins, etcetera, things favoured by refugees from East Europe or soldiers returning home.

"I wish you wouldn't buy them gherkins," my Mother told me. "They stinks the cupboard out."

You now heard of people who boiled their own spaghetti or macaroni, rather than buy it in Heinz tins with tomato sauce, as before. Powdered coffee replaced the bottles of coffee essence, and some people actually started using tea bags. Pre-packaging became common: it was not long before sweets began to appear in plastic bags, replacing the great glass jars used in the shops when sweets were weighed by hand. Ball-pointed pens went on sale at fantastic prices. Shoes appeared with 'composite' rather than good leather soles, presaging the end of Beale's shoe repair shop near Hafod Bridge. The first 'self-service' stores opened: you could actually go around and take things off the shelves yourself. My Auntie Doris, an innocuous soul if ever there was one, got confused (or so she said) and walked out without paying. The police caught her, and she came up before the Swansea magistrates.

"There's awful, isn't it?" said Gran. "We've never had anything like that in the family before!"

When you saw Auntie Doris in the street afterwards she would give you a sort of shame-faced smile. If everything had been safely behind a counter there would have been no temptation.

Transport began to improve. The Corporation horses which pulled the dust carts disappeared, as did the steam rollers and steam lorries (though Scotty – the greengrocer – still came around with his cart). Florry Luxton's son-in-law (who wasted no money on drink) bought an old car: Stan Jones, who lived next door down to us, asked whether he could sit in the driver's seat, just to try the upholstery.

The last gas-mantle users, including my Auntie Enid, went onto the electric mains, and people got rid of wireless sets worked by wet batteries. We had a gas point fitted near the fireplace in the kitchen, so that we could use one of the new gas pokers and light the fire even if the firewood was damp. The first television sets, with three or four-inch screens, went on sale, but we never had one. My cousin Donald up in Treboeth got a tape recorder in an enormous cabinet to help him practice his acting (by this time he dreamed of going on the stage). When I went up to Treboeth to see it I heard my voice recorded for the first time, and thought I sounded wonderful. In the back gardens the last chickens were slaughtered for the oven.

★ ★ ★

Another change was the re-appearance of Campbell's noble paddle steamers – the Bristol Channel was now free of mines. So a few weeks after I got out of hospital I was able to fulfil a long-held dream, and make a proper deep sea voyage – in other words, a day's outing to Ilfracombe on the *Glen Gower*. I went with my Mother, for there was still no hope of my Father taking me anywhere. It was a glorious sunny morning, with, however, something of a breeze off the coast. The boat left from a wharf near the mouth of the Tawe, just below the town bridge. All the seats on deck were taken, so I had to lean against the rail, but no matter, it was wonderful to be on board. After years of reading sea stories, I was to sail the seas myself, with a magnificent steam engine, easily viewed, below decks.

When the *Glen Gower* cast off, everyone was in good spirits and looked forward to a marvellous day. Unfortunately, the breeze was stronger than anticipated, and the ship heaved a great deal. As the morning advanced, however, the motion got stronger, and passengers started to be sick. Inexperienced in the ways of the sea, some chose to lose their breakfasts on the windward side of the vessel. So regurgitated food was blown across the deck onto the rest of us in a mild but awful drizzle. I had no sea legs, but fortunately was not much affected.

"Oh Gawd," said my Mother, trying to shield herself with her mack, "there's terrible, isn' it? Let's go below!"

Down in the bar they were selling people brandy to calm their stomachs, but my Mother and I didn't have any. There was widespread relief when the ship at last tied up at Ilfracombe. The day there passed uneventfully – the main thing for me being the paddle steamer. Fortunately, the sea was much calmer going back, and no one, as far as I could see, was sea-sick. Looking back, I thought the voyage was absolutely glorious – despite the digestive element.

★ ★ ★

"The spivs are here again," John Lewis told me one day. "Let's go down and see them!"

"Spivs?" I said. "What are spivs?"

"They sell you things. Down on the bomb site near the market. Come on."

The centre of Swansea had been devastated, and when the rubble was cleared large empty places remained. Some of them were occupied, on fine afternoons, by furniture vans which came down from London loaded with a goods for sale. John led me to one near the Market. The salesmen – the 'spivs' – were in their best suits, and seemed very persistent. One of them clambered on to the back of his vehicle.

"Good afternoon, ladies and gentlemen," he announced in raucous cockney. "We're art experts from London and we've got something special for you today." (Aside: "Sid, let's have a couple"). Sid pulled two objects wrapped in newspaper from a packing case, and his colleague unwrapped them. They were a pair of alabaster figurines, roughly painted, as you could see from the crowd, if you looked carefully. He placed them reverently on another packing case which served as a demonstration table.

"A beautiful shepherd boy and a shepherd girl," he cried "what a lovely pair, I wonder what they was doing in the hay, though? Ha, ha... But just think, ladies and gentlemen [a trace of awe appeared in his voice] if this pair of ornaments looks so beautiful on this old packing case, what are they going to look like on the sideboard in your parlour?" After a meaningful pause he continued "Normally these ornaments are on sale at ten pounds a pair in the poshest shops in London, (you know, Selfridges and Harrods, with all the showcases and glitter), but not here, ladies and gentlemen, not here. For you, today," he suddenly raised his voice, full blast "only five bob each, the pair for nine and six!"

One or two old ladies, the neat, house-proud type from the Swansea valley, fell for it straight away, and fumbled in their purses.

"That lady over there would like one, Sid. A very wise purchase, madam. They'll keep you company while you're reading your bible. And another here, the people recognises a bargain when they sees one!"

A couple of assistant spivs unpacked a lot more, to give the impression of a lively sale, but John and I could see that the extra ones were just being passed back behind the van, out of sight. We exchanged meaningful glances. I had never seen anything like it before. What a waste of good money! But the spivs were fun to watch on a Saturday afternoon, and we saw many.

* * *

Auntie Annie came down one Wednesday to clean for Gran, as usual. "Brenda is very upset," she said. Brenda was a distant cousin of mine, though I could never quite work out how. She lived in Lisbon Terrace, like Betty. "She had a real shock."

"What was that then?" Gran asked.

"Well, she met this American airman called Wilberforce at an air force dance in Fairwood Common, and they started going out together. To tell you the truth, she took it they were courting, and she hoped he was going to ask her to marry him and take her back to O-hi-o, where his home was. She started having him back home for meals. Auntie Martha liked him too, and they thought he felt really at home with them."

"Oh."

"Then one evening he forgot himself. They was having a cup of tea in the kitchen, and without thinking he mentioned this woman back in O-hi-O, it was obvious that it was his missus. There was a terrible silence after he said it, they was all so embarrassed, but it was too late, the truth was out. Brenda cried her eyes out after he left, and that was the end of the romance. She said she would never trust an American soldier again. I don't think anything went on between them, mind. They were only going out together for a year. Thank Gawd for that!"

* * *

Starting back at Dynevor was just as unpleasant as starting at the other schools I had attended, and my heart was heavy. When I got there I found that little had changed – the staff was the same, the atmosphere was the same, and plaster was still peeling.

Indeed, to begin with, life was worse: the Fourth Form they put me into was much less hospitable than the Third had been. Mr Cox was very much in evidence and wanted me to go straight into the Fifths, which was the School Certificate year, but I was not sure I could manage the work, and I ended up in 4E, the class for the less academic boys intending to leave early. I was still a non-fighter, wobbly on my feet, and incapable of sport. So it took only a few days for the bullying to restart, though more subtly than hitherto. Threats of physical violence were replaced by concerted efforts to make things awkward for me. For example, each of us had a desk with a lid and a padlock for keeping books in. One day I got to school to find that my lock had been wired up so as to be almost unopenable, while my classmates waited gleefully to see me struggling with it. I had to take my tin shears to school for several days afterwards in case they wired it again.

The tedium of my remaining four years at Dynevor is best left undescribed, though there were a few lighter moments. I was now really too old to sing in the choir, but they stuck me in somehow, and I took part in another concert in the Brangwyn Hall. The French language strengthened its grip on my mentality, and Gran still enjoyed listening to the stories I translated. Homework, much of it interesting, was taking up an ever greater part of the evening, though there was hardly anywhere for me to study. The marble-topped washstand in the front bedroom was low and cold for the elbows, but I managed somehow. In the winter months I would plug our brown-stained electric fire into a light-socket adaptor, and on a few occasions I lit a fire in the bedroom grate, though it was a time-consuming business. On the whole my studies at Dynevor went fairly well, and when the School Certificate results came out I found that I had got four Gs and four Cs, the equivalent, I think, of As and Bs in today's GCSEs. A few boys had done better, many worse.

At least there was no difficulty about my going on the Sixth Form. My Mother was proud and delighted, and made no mention of the financial burden she was carrying.

"I'm very happy to see you getting on so well, Mervyn," she would say. One day you will probably have a good job."

Formerly she had helped me with my arithmetic, but now I needed no such assistance as I had chosen English, Geography and French. My elevation to the Sixths meant that the bullying stopped, but it was, alas, replaced by another problem. One day Mr. Cox came up to me in the corridor.

"Mervyn," he said, "some good news!"

"Oh, really, Sir," I said.

"They've made you a Prefect."

"Oh, have they, Sir! What a surprise!"

"Oh, my Gawd," I thought and my heart sank, though I managed to utter a word of thanks. Mr. Cox had proposed me with the best of intentions, hoping to improve my chances of getting a place at a university. He could not have comprehended my fears.

They'll put me on the gate to check the lates, I thought. I can never stand up against so-and-so, or so-and-so, if they challenge me to a fight! (In fact one did, and I had to make an ignominious retreat.) Then I'll have to take my turn at reading the lesson in front of the whole school in Mount Pleasant.

In fact I did not sleep a wink the night before my turn came up and though I managed it somehow I was a bag of nerves. How I wished I could be as self-confident as Peter Macpherson, whose father kept a shop in Oxford Street, and could tough anything out. He had been made a prefect, too.

Eventually the day came when Mr. W. Bryn Thomas called each of the Sixth formers into his study, and asked them about their plans for a career.

"Now, m'boy," said the Headmaster, looking at me intently under his lined forehead. "What do you intend to do after you have finished your Highers?"

"I've applied to do Russian at Manchester University, Sir," I said. I'd gone for Manchester because it was a good, accessible university; given my modest background and my lack of prowess in sport, Oxford and Cambridge were out of the question. I had also made enquiries at the School of Slavonic Studies in London, but they showed no interest.

"Russian?" said Mr. Thomas, incredulously. "Russian? Why on earth should you choose that? No one from Dynevor has ever done Russian."

In fact I could hardly explain it myself: the only Russian person I had ever, to my knowledge, met was the unsavoury Mr. Kramsky, and I had scarcely spoken to him. I had certainly never heard a word of the language.

"Well, Sir," I said, "there is a Cold War on and I thought it might be useful. I don't know anyone else studying it. And I like languages."

Mr. Thomas regained his composure.

"A very wise choice, I'm sure," he said, with the lost air of one who knew nothing about it. "There must be fine prospects there! Work hard! I hope you get a place at Manchester. Let me know what happens when the results come out. Call the next boy in, will you?"

★ ★ ★

Inevitably, after the breakthrough at Hill House, sex reared its wondrous head, and quite often. Jack, I recalled, had almost got married to a Greek girl when he was in Egypt, and I knew that although no great womaniser, he was still having It. He was careless enough to leave some latex items in the drawer of the marble-topped washstand. It was the first time I had seen them, enclosed in silver packets. Whenever Jack mentioned It he grinned and made a slight tickling motion, waist-level, with the fingers of his right hand.

'It' was not easy to cope with after I left hospital, in fact the entire picture was unsatisfactory. At first there was still hardly anyone I could confide in. John Lewis was very reserved about it, though he did tell me, with a grin, that a girl living near him in Mayhill had come up when he was sitting on the wall, and grabbed his unmentionable. No doubt she was attracted by his good looks, some of the girls were like that... Normally, you only talked about It if you had an exploit to boast about, and I knew no easy girls who might serve for practice – even if I could overcome my shyness. Immediate relief was all right, but you were left with a guilty feeling afterwards. And Baden Powell had intimated that if you indulged in 'beastliness' you weren't being a Man. In the diary which I was keeping at the time I asked occasionally God to help me restrain my urges.

Of course, I knew that other boys were having It. Donald's tough friend Malcom, who was an apprentice fitter, would brag about doing It with his girlfriend Milly. He told me how, one night, she had taken him home late, when her family was abed, and given herself up to him on a coconut mat on the kitchen floor.

"I was up 'er for fifteen minutes by their clock on the mantelpiece," said Malcom, carefully avoiding bad language.

Later he found out that someone else had also been "up 'er", and he declared that if he ever met this bloke there would be a fight. "I don' blame 'im, mind," he added charitably. "She's a randy little piece". They got married later.

My cousin Donald was having It, too – in fact we began to drift apart precisely because he was becoming so preoccupied. He was turning into a handsome youth, sociable and attractive to women, and he knew places where you could find them. When I discovered that he had begun to lead a marvellous, sex-orientated life, I was green with envy. He was much taken with a pretty little thing called Ruby, who was from Townhill and wore lipstick.

He told me in lurid detail how Ruby and her sister had once taken him to the Carlton Cinema, and (one sitting on each side) brought him to a climax in the middle of main feature. "Gawd, It was wonderful, mun," he said. "Messy, though." When, one afternoon, we went up to Felindre together on our bikes, and he actually left early in order to get back to her, I realised that in comparison my company was of no interest whatever. The fact that Donald was not very good at school and had no hope of doing Highers paled into insignificance against the splendour of his sexual adventures. I had to wait a bit before I had any myself.

★ ★ ★

Relations between my Mother and Father were still in a dismal state. The situation over in Osterley Street had in fact deteriorated, in so far as Gamma was getting weaker, and my Father was having ever more trouble with his chest. His work had not picked up, yet he would not consider any other job (he was about fifty, in any case). My Mother was still trying to get him back, and even meeting him occasionally, though I no longer joined them. The maintenance allowance was still a problem – as indeed was Ada. Eight and a half years after he left Aberdyberthi Street, my Mother wrote to him, on the 5th December, 1949

> Dear Billie,
> I think my patience has endured long enough. Under the new Act, I am entitled to approximately 3 times as much as the 27 shillings which you allow me. On each occasion I have been to the court, you have made it necessary, owing to the fact that you would not cooperate.
>   I am prepared to carry on as I am on one condition. That is, that you break your associations with Ada Dyer and see me, if only once a week. I want to try and hold you in respectability for Mervyn's name sake. He is your legitimate son and you owe that much to him. I do not wish to see fingers pointed at him through your association with the low woman.
>   Think over what I have said. Before proceeding [to court] I should like to see you. Outside the Rialto at 8 o'oclock on Saturday would do me. I shall be there. Nobody need know.
>   It is my final offer to you. If you accept as I said before, I shall carry on as now, though God knows it is a struggle. If you do not see the reason of my request I'm afraid Miss Dyer will prove a very expensive luxury.
>   Sincerely yours, Lil.

My Mother's use of the word 'legitimate' could only have been a reference to Doreen's illegitimacy, otherwise 'your son' or 'your own son' would have been adequate: and obviously, she knew that Ada was unmarried. She did not, however, take my Father to court, and a few weeks later again tried to meet him.

If the [shift] numbers show that you are not working Saturday afternoon, I shall wait for you at 8 o'clock by the Rialto.

I still feel the same about things as I did when I wrote to you about five weeks ago. That is, that if we cannot see each other for an hour or so on Saturdays, I must apply to have my allowance increased. Why should I have to apply for grants and charity in order to keep Mervyn in school at the same time knowing that you are pubbing with that Danygraig Ada. You deny it but I can believe my own eyes...

Yours sincerely, Lil

Yes, my Mother was still doing a bit of snooping, in fact I had once, quite by chance, seen her shadowing my Father near the 'Midland' pub at the main docks entrance. She was no detective and looked rather ridiculous, craning her neck and dodging behind passers-by. And she certainly knew what Ada looked like: on one occasion (Enid told me years later) my Mother and Enid had got on a bus together near the market, only to find my Father's paramour sitting on one of the front seats. Ada turned round and laughed.

"Yes, it's me" she cried, pointing at herself.

My Mother never mentioned Ada's name in my hearing, and I remained blissfully ignorant of the existence of both mother and daughter. But the angry tone of the January letter portended a break, albeit partial, in her silence. One day, when I was, I imagine, just over sixteen, I ventured to make some rather favourable comment about my Father – nothing very important, but enough to provoke another burst of hysterics.

"Let me tell you now," my Mother shouted, "that your Father stopped your child maintenance allowance the day of your sixteenth birthday, even though you are still at Dynevor. What do you think of that? And he has been running around Swansea with a common prostitute."

I don't know how she expected me to react, probably she thought the news would be devastating, even without reference to a half-sister. But she was wrong. The disappearance of meagre paternal support had made no palpable difference to my life, and I took it all for granted, as before. We always seemed to have just enough money to manage on – thanks to my Mother's careful house keep-ing. On the other hand, I knew my Father had always been 'pubbing', and the news that he was running around with another woman just about fitted his ever more paltry image. He had always been so mean towards me (witness the tools, watch, and camera incidents, for example) that I never expected much from him.

So I turned away from her in silence, more concerned, I suppose, to avoid a row. And only once did my Mother herself ever comment on her own performance in life.

"I've made a terrible mess of it, son, haven't I?" she said, sadly.

* * *

A gleam of sunlight was, however, to appear on her joyless horizon, in the form of a highly advantageous injury to her person. She had always dreamed of owning No. 64, paying no rent, and keeping the parlour as a little showroom, like everybody else in the street. But there was no hope of finding the money needed, and Gran's bed was in the parlour, anyway. Then one morning, as my Mother was crossing Jersey Street on her way to work, a van backed up without warning and knocked her over. She was bruised and shaken, though not seriously hurt; and being a somewhat pugnacious creature had the presence of mind to go up to Doctor O'Kane's surgery up Greenhill and get him to note the bruising. Shortly afterwards she made a claim against the van's insurance company, which she had managed to locate, perhaps with the help of the driver.

A few days later, as she told me subsequently, a neatly dressed man came to see her at the office. He was from the insurance, and shortly after offered her a full twenty pounds in cash (about a month's wage) if she would settle there and then. She refused, and got the good doctor to state that the injury might well give rise to arthritis in later life. As a result, the company ran scared, and offered a magnificent settlement of four hundred pounds, which she promptly accepted.

With the proceeds in the bank my Mother sent me down to ask Auntie Kate about buying No. 64. I found her, as usual, sitting at her sewing machine: since Uncle Gilbert died, she made a living as a seamstress. To start off with she was quite pleasant, but when I mentioned the leaking roof, the terrible damp in the back kitchen and the bedroom window frame which almost fell out every time you opened it, she got angry, and I could see the muscles tightening in her neck. An altercation started. I recalled, for good measure, how mean her father had been in Lamb Street, and her request for rent the morning after the bombing. I may have made a cheeky reference to ill-fitting corsets (she was an ungainly women), though I later regretted doing so, for her corsetry was really no concern of mine, even in the heat of the moment. The meeting finished, need I add, with no agreement in sight. All her kindness to me while I was in hospital had been forgotten.

No. 64 had all been in the same sorry state as long as I could remember – Gran, with her mild nature, had adamantly refused to ask Auntie Kate to repair anything, so as not to spoil relations. But my Mother was not one to let an opportunity for a good row to pass, and on hearing of Auntie Kate's response promptly took me back down to continue the battle in Auntie Kate's passage. My Mother had, however, acquired a trump card: she had heard that the Corporation had gained the power to issue 'dilapidation schedules' and oblige a landlord to have extensive repairs done – out of his or her own pocket.

"I would like to have a roof that didn't leak, and dry walls and a parlour like yours," said my Mother, boldly throwing open Auntie Kate's parlour door.

"Oh, you jealous cat," said Auntie Kate.

"And I'm going down to the Corporation to ask about a dilapidation schedule," my Mother continued.

"All right, go on, then."

That seemed to be the end of the matter, but Auntie Kate was visibly shaken. Though reluctant to forgo the ten-and-six a week rent, she was terrified of the Corporation and its schedules. A little later she sent word to say that she would sell the house for three hundred pounds, which was the going price in the street. So as a result of all this my Mother ended up with part, at least, of her dream realised, and the prospect, in the longer run, of hot water and a bathroom, like Auntie Annie in Treboeth. My Mother, incidentally, was to suffer from various maladies in later life, but never arthritis.

★ ★ ★

I suppose the real end of my boyhood in Swansea came one morning in October, 1951 when, in the company of three classmates from Dynevor, I boarded the maroon-liveried L.M.S. train which was to take us to Manchester. After getting reasonable results in my Higher School Certificate I had indeed been accepted to study Russian there. We had a compartment to ourselves and spirits were high, because we were on the threshold of an exciting new life. The train panted its way along Swansea Bay, up Clyne Valley, and on through the green Welsh hills. But there was another surprise awaiting me.

Just before leaving my Mother and Gran at No. 64 I had received an envelope addressed to me in Jack's hand, but I had not had time to open it. Withdrawing for a moment from the banter and jollity in the compartment, I read the opening sentence.

Dear Mervyn,
I think the time has now come for me to tell you that I am your brother.

At first I did not take his words in. What was he on about? "I am your brother". Was it a joke? The letter (it was a short one) went on to say that everything was in fact the same between us, and that we would no doubt remain on very good terms. He was illegitimate by another father, but had not been told himself until he was sixteen. Uncle Glyn had given him the news...

My first thought was one of pleasure at having a brother – or half-brother – since all my life I had thought I was an only child. He was quite right about personal relations being the same. Yet as I looked through the carriage window that morning I realised that I had lighted upon another pool of sadness in the family history, namely, the ignominy and pain which my Mother must have endured when she bore an illegitimate child in the 'twenties.

Much of her erratic behaviour, right from the Lamb Street days, now became comprehensible to me – her unsociability, unwilling-ness to mix, her feeling of being different, her passion for betterment. She had passed much of this on to me: Jack, brought up as her brother, had largely escaped it. Any hope she had had for a better life had been blighted by a few minutes of physical contact with a man who would let her down. Why had she done it? Was she in love, or had she hoped to win a husband who could give her a life beyond the Hafod? Had she been seduced for her beauty? Perhaps the fact that she had borne an illegitimate child drew her closer to Billie Matthews, who had fathered one himself. Gran, for all of her kindness, may have treated her badly when the pregnancy became known, creating a fund of bitterness which welled up when she, Gran, was old and weak.

Such were my thoughts as the steam engine hauled us through the hills and dales, stopping at picturesque little stations I had never heard of. At one of the stops, after we had been travelling for a couple of hours, a woman in a white apron got on, lugging an enor-mous basket of thick cups, jugs of tea and milk, Salvation army style.

"Anyone want tea, boys?" asked one of my companions. "Anyone brought sandwiches?"

★ ★ ★

The news, though startling, was to some extent marginalised by the exigencies of the moment – my arrival in Manchester, moving into new digs, registering at the Russian Department, and so on. After reflecting for a while I decided not to write to my Mother, and in the weeks that followed I experienced a growing feeling of resentment about the way things had turned out. The fact that she had borne a child outside marriage troubled me not one iota. What I did find devastating was the fact that she had never told me about it! She had allowed me to grow into manhood without my knowing that Jack was a half-brother, not an Uncle at all. When I returned to Swansea for Christmas I demonstratively stopped speaking to her. She was very upset and promptly blamed Jack for telling me. But it was too delicate a matter ever to be properly discussed between us, and she never understood the specific reason for my anger.

"Some women," she told me bitterly, on the sole occasion when the matter was mentioned, "had more than one child outside marriage. I was never 'common'."

A few months were to pass before the hurt eased a little, and there was some reconciliation. I realised that (after all was said and done) she had only been trying to protect me. I was still unaware, of course, that my Father had doubled up with a half-sister. Astonishing also was the care with which my Mother's secret had been kept by everyone around. My cousin Audrey, Donald's elder sister, told me later that she had found out about it not from a family member of our family, but from her husband Harry, after she got married. Harry happened to be friendly with Jack, and had learnt it from him directly. Jack was a decade older than I; if I had worked out the ages (which I never did) I would have found that Gran's husband died years before Jack was born, and Gran was probably too old to bear children anyway. Over all the years of my boyhood there was only one tiny incident which might have alerted me to the truth, namely, Elsie Morris's reference to my 'brother' when she was showing me her mother's corpse. Surprised at so strange an error, I had "corrected" her and thought no more of it.

Jack, when I next saw him, filled in some of the details – as a matter of fact, he had gone to a lot of trouble to elucidate them.

"Our Mother," he told me, "was seduced by a solicitor called Whitfield, a married man who lived in Bridgend. (How strange the 'our' sounded, I had always said 'my'.) Apparently he asked her to come and look after his children in the evenings. When she got pregnant there was no question of marriage, and she must have suffered terribly. She told me she hid her condition as long as she could, by 'binding herself up'! She went off to some place in Somerset to give birth, but I don't know the details... I remember one day, when I was still very small, Gran and Auntie Sal took me to a house with a green front door, and showed me to the man who opened it. He did not ask us in. It must have been Whitfield's house in Bridgend. I suppose Gran and Auntie Sal hoped that Whitfield would help with some money, but as far as I know, he never paid a penny towards my upkeep. Nobody seemed to doubt the paternity, but there was no question of taking it up in court. We were too poor."

* * *

Reflections on years gone by can generate their own pleasure, even when they contain much sadness. Like most boys in their late teens I was more concerned with the future than with the past, though the past had already laid an indelible imprint on me. Many of the people who had a role to play in my life later were living their own lives in America, Russia and other parts of the world, hardly aware that Swansea, let alone the Hafod, existed. But I must add a few words more on what happened in my own little circle.

Some kindly faces were soon to disappear, grandparents first. By the time I left for Manchester Gran began complaining about an unaccustomed limpness in her arms. Months passed, and gradually it got worse, and in the autumn of 1954 my Mother and Auntie Annie decided that she could be better looked after in Treboeth. I well remember her tears as I helped her out of the house, leaning heavily on her walking stick. Uncle Glyn's car was waiting outside. She was quite certain that she was leaving her home for the very last time, and my attempts to console her were of no avail.

I went up to see her before taking the train back to the University. Confined to bed in the parlour, she seemed to be reconciled to death. The curtains were partly drawn: I embraced her in the half-light and left, her last words, "Good bye, son" ringing in my ears. She died quietly in her sleep a few days later. Auntie Annie was sitting with her when her breathing stopped.

Within a few months Gamma in St. Thomas succumbed to an intestinal cancer which had been developing for years. Once, after a particularly bad bout of pain, she had developed a death rattle, prompting my Auntie Ethel (or so it was said) to pull a winding sheet out of the bottom drawer. But miraculously (for Auntie Ethel was a fervent Christian Scientist) she had rallied, and on that occasion the drawer regained its lugubrious content. I was in Swansea for both funerals, one in the long-awaited peace of Cwmgelli Cemetery, and the other in Danygraig, in fact hard by Ada's house. Young and resilient, I grieved over both departings: but there is no doubt whose image was to remain closest to my heart.

In Swansea, my Father's world inevitably fell apart. My visits to Osterley Street, where he now lived alone, got rarer, I was in Manchester most of the time, anyway. He was retired from the coal-trimmers association after mis-managing a ship at the quayside, and causing, I believe, a certain amount of collision damage. Coal dust and life-long smoking had given him emphysema, and he hardly had enough breath to walk, let alone gallivant. I presume Ada's presence faded. After 1950 my Mother and Father stopped their evening meetings altogether; there was, I imagine, little point in them, as age told. My Father died in hospital in 1962, lodged there because in his last few days he was too weak and breathless to look after himself. My kind Uncle Emrys, who was now keeping a small shop close by, helped with the funeral arrangements, and after the cremation handed me a small pack of pocket books, tattered documents, and my Mother's letters – all that my Father had left. I leafed through them quickly and put them away, without realising the secrets they contained.

I don't think I ever told my Mother I had them: perhaps it was better thus. With Gran's death, she got her 'little palace', albeit as grimy as ever, to herself, with a proper front parlour and bathroom extension built on. She managed, in her last years, to find a contentment that had eluded her throughout her sad life. She developed a liver cancer and died at our house in London in January, 1971, as I slept on a couch beside her. She was seventy years of age. She was coughing bile and very uncomfortable.

"Well, I want to go," she said bravely, a few hours before she lost consciousness. "I've had my three score years and ten."

Elsie Morris passed away shortly after my Mother, at the age of seventy three: Auntie Beatrice sort of faded from view after my Father's days, and I never saw her again. Enid, dear Enid, seemed to change little: after seeing off Jack Thomas, she went on as before, living Hafod-fashion in No. 58. She died at the ripe age of 85, surrounded by her family.

* * *

Looking around at my own generation, there was vigorous change as young men turned into adults. Gerald Peachey had disappeared into the greyness of his beloved Scunthorpe, and found a job in a shoe-shop. His Auntie told my Mother, when they met one day, that he had lost the sight of one of his eyes, but was managing well enough. When I ran across John Dermady, I discovered a quiet young man engrossed in an accountancy course. John Halfpenny left Dynevor early, and tried to become a motor mechanic, but the oil fumes aggravated his asthma, and he took a job as a bus conductor instead. When I saw him briefly, a year or two later, he exhibited a flushed enthusiasm for cadet training in the Royal Air Force. Donny Thomas learnt his trade as a painter, in the family's good proletarian tradition. Brinley Clifford I observed one day hot-footing it up Carmarthen Road. He was, he told me breathlessly, on the trail of a good 'story' – the *Evening Post* had taken him on as a cub reporter.

My cousin Donald, despite the combined efforts of my Uncle Glyn and his private school, failed to acquire a taste for learning, and after a period of national service in Malaya attempted to become a film extra in London. He only got one speaking part ever – as a policeman in a court scene, when he had to shout "Silence in court!" He ended up as a teacher. John Lewis, perhaps the cleverest boy I knew, had gone to a secretarial college (all his parents could afford) and started work as a railway clerk. He loved pursuing friendly arguments in the office when the train movements got too boring. My friend Michael went up to Oxford to read law – at one of the less prestigious colleges, it is true, – but still Oxford. "I should have gone to Magdalene," he once told me modestly. We were to remain friends for many years.

Jack took a job as a teacher at World's End in Chelsea, but went on painting, and (since he was so likeable) was absorbed into an arty-farty crowd in London. He did his best to keep up with them, and successfully suppressed his Hafod accent whenever he remembered. He published a couple of small books, including a biography of Van Gogh, *The Man who Loved the Sun*, and sold dozens of paintings. One of the peaks of his career was a half-hour show of his canvasses on television, which he presented personally. Most of his work was in a Lowry style, including two pictures hung in the Glynn Vivian Art Gallery in Swansea. Yet the tragedy of the Jones family was to cast its shadow on him, too: he endured an unhappy marriage and fathered a mentally retarded child. He passed away at 71 after a long and painful illness. Unexpectedly, towards the end of his life he found unexpected peace and solace in the Roman Catholic Church.

REFLECTIONS AT A CEREMONY

It is a little after three o'clock on Thursday, the 7th July, 1955, and a large crowd of people – parents, teachers, and university staff – has just been admitted to the Whitworth Hall on Manchester University campus. They have come to see the annual conferment of degrees, in which I am due to take part.

It is a fine afternoon, but a hundred fireplaces in the terraced houses of Moss Side lend a smoky smell to the air. Outside the hall lines of students, feeling more than slightly self-conscious in their newly-donned gowns, hoods and mortar boards, are ready to file into the hall and receive, with due ceremony, a sheet of good quality paper confirming their status as Bachelors of the University. I am somewhere amongst them.

At last the order comes to advance; we enter the porch with as much decorum as we can muster, no fun and jokes now. The architecture is only mock Gothic, but the sense of solemnity is genuine enough. Inside the hall we find an organ playing, and an impressive line of dignitaries, even more elaborately be-gowned than ourselves, sitting on a platform at the end. The body of the hall is packed with our relatives and friends, though seats in the front have been left for us. As the procession moves forward, I catch sight of my Mother and Father sitting together near the central aisle. My Mother is wide-eyed with emotion; she cannot take her gaze off me for a second. My Father, frail and breathing with difficulty, manages a wan smile. How she persuaded him to come to Manchester (just for the day, of course) I cannot imagine.

The ceremony proceeds as in years past. The 'graduands' are called to the platform, one by one, to receive a degree. A white-haired old professor from Archangel rises to propose me, in heavily accented English, for an Honours degree in Russian. I go up to receive the certificate, and enjoy a few seconds of prominence; the medics sitting in the gallery give the cheer reserved for the prettiest girls and the University's best degrees; a few paper streamers fly through the air, and there is even a puff of flour. But for my Mother the event is serious indeed, dreamed of through many miserable years.

Not a great deal happens afterwards. We all wander back out onto the campus. My Mother, breaking the habit of a lifetime, insists on my having an expensive photograph taken, so as to register my appearance in academic dress. I know she wants it to adorn the parlour for the rest of her days. I think the idea is silly, but somehow manage a smile. With that over, and in deference to my taste for curry, the three of us go to a cheap Indian restaurant nearby. My Father orders English roast lamb and potatoes, but the gravy has curry in it, so he can hardly eat it. I suspect he can ill afford it, anyway. Later my parents take the bus for London Road railway station. No, there is no need for me to go all the way into town with them. They have had a marvellous day.

It was the last time the three of us were together.